Senseless and Sensitivity

misprints required a corrected edition

Senseless and Sensitivity

Robert Charles Jones, who left behind autobiographical poetry and journals, and his biographer and father, Bartlett C. Jones

iUniverse, Inc.
New York Lincoln Shanghai

Senseless and Sensitivity

All Rights Reserved © 2004 by Bartlett C. Jones

No part of this book may be reproduced or transmitted in any form or by any means, graphic, electronic, or mechanical, including photocopying, recording, taping, or by any information storage retrieval system, without the written permission of the publisher.

iUniverse, Inc.

For information address:
iUniverse, Inc.
2021 Pine Lake Road, Suite 100
Lincoln, NE 68512
www.iuniverse.com

ISBN: 0-595-32623-4

Printed in the United States of America

Although he adopted a gay lifestyle in college, Robert Charles Jones, actor and aspiring poet, had numerous female friends. (The female illustrations for this memorial are his sketches and costume ideas.)

Besides loving parents, he left many close friends and grieving relatives.

This book is dedicated to them all, and to anyone who entertains the belief that a sinful, self-destructive person may also possess noble qualities and aspirations.

CONTENTS

FOREWORD ix
I. L.A. BUS LIFE 1
II. MELANCHOLIC VISIONS (1968–1986) 9
III. COLLEGE YEARS: RATIONAL OBSERVATIONS: ACCEPTANCE OF GAY LIFESTYLE 45
IV. CHICAGO YEARS: ANOMIE AND HEARTBREAK ...76
V. ON TOUR: ACTING KUDOS; MORAL RUIN 91
VI. L.A.: LOVELORN LAMENTS IN SURREAL SETTINGS 120
VII. HOMOEROTICISM AND DESPAIR 169
VIII. CRISIS, GRIEF, GUILT, & HEALING 200

FOREWORD

When I left my dying son's apartment in Los Angeles to return to Missouri, I took all of his manuscript poems and journals that I could find. His close friend since college days later gave me a disc containing his early poems and more journals. Arranged chronologically, Rob's poetry became a poignant autobiography best understood through the journals. (One of the poems won an art-league prize; three have been published by the Columbia Chapter of the Missouri Writers Guild. See "In November," "Breaking the Surface," and "Who Stole Me?" Well Versed 2001.)

A sympathetic editor looked at sample poems and journal excerpts, and suggested another dimension. The material needed an overview. Since depicting a promising life cut short by AIDS has been overdone, the book should be about healing as well as death and dying. I should be the primary editor and interject myself into the narrative because I knew more about the material than any professional editor could take the time to learn, and I was the expert on my own healing.

I was devastated that Rob died so young and ashamed that he had random, unprotected sex without having tests for HIV and AIDS. The following short story, which I began on long bus trips between his apartment and the hospital where he lay in a coma, launched my coping with grief and guilt.

Gratitude for the love and good times we shared welled up as I shaped the story; the patterns of bus conduct diverted me from my certain bereavement and reminded me that human experiences, expressed through the arts, were rich enough to justify a positive approach to life.

I had a purpose in mastering the bus system. Rob had been very indignant that I didn't buy him a car after he settled in Los Angeles following an extended nationwide tour with a theatre company presenting homosexual porn. (He, and later his friend, said that he couldn't attend auditions or get a job in L.A. without a car.)

Recalling how he reduced the car he drove in college to a shambles, his defaults on lease obligations, and his years of underemployment and substance abuse, I didn't want to invest in a car unless he had enough income to keep it insured and running. I was certain the bus system would suffice in the meantime.

Rob had bitterly responded that I didn't know L.A. Now, however, I found it easy to get about by bus—particularly if you got up early in the morning. I even took a trip to a Social Security Office ironically located on the Hollywood "Walk of Fame." (It's eerie to apply for benefits you doubt your actor son will live to collect and then step on a memorial star dedicated to Marilyn Monroe.) Each time the buses passed a theatre playhouse, I felt less guilty.

Because I had control of his life for so long, it's hard to lose a loving son with considerable talent, charm and excellent health without wondering how you failed as a parent. But through the years of wondering—pricked by multifaceted, crippling guilt, I never regretted refusing to buy Rob that car. But the story shows how deeply he was wounded by lack of a car—perhaps to the core of his self image. And the book will show that lack of self-esteem can lead to self-destruction.

I.

L.A. BUS LIFE

On the bus trip to get my dying son's cat euphonized, some passengers smiled.
"Nice kitty, kitty."
"She's female," a woman said, though the cat was barely visible through the bars of the carrying-case. "Hi, kitty. What's your name?"
"Kate," I said.
"Taking her to the hospital for a shot?"
"That's it."
"Takin' good care of her," an African American woman said.
"She's sweet," another woman said. "I know you'll always give her a good home."
"Thanks." I hadn't enjoyed such public approval since attacking our Vietnam War role at a college rally 30 years ago. And again, I was the only Anglo on the bus. Why hadn't I kept records on that since I began riding the L.A. buses three weeks ago—a great conversation piece when I got back to Missouri?
"Which way to L Street?" I asked the driver just before we reached my stop. "I'm going to the animal hospital."
"Can't help you," she said, then shouted, "Anybody know where L Street is?"
"I show you," a girl—maybe a Thai or Filipino—said. She steadied me when I lurched getting up.

"I'll make it," I said, milking my limp from a pinched sciatic nerve by flourishing my cane and swinging the carrying-case.

"Take your time," the driver said. "I'm watching out for you."

"Thanks." I chuckled at the passengers' comments. They didn't know that incontinent Kate fouled floors, closet corners, baseboards—even window sills, that I was taking her to be executed.

"I show you." The girl's breast-length hair rippled when she cocked her head. After she guided me across the street, she took the carrying-case. "I go by hospital."

I followed her, then untruthfully told the hospital staff that my son had approved the euthanasia. On the way back to the bus stop, I wondered how hard it would be to get to a 70 or 71 bus to the L.A. County Hospital—whose facade flashes on TV screens to introduce "General Hospital" episodes. Boarding a bus for downtown, I asked the driver, "How close do you go to 7th and Spring?"

"I go right there." The genial, heavy African American male grinned. It was pleasant riding his bus. He let disabled riders reach a seat before starting ahead, and called out the stops. Looking at a park playground was a welcome relief from miles of shops. But then I flashed back to happy hours pushing my son in a swing.

A heavy lady got on and tried unsuccessfully to force herself into a narrow space on the bench seat reserved for the disabled. "People are harassing me," she shouted. "I don't like people pushing me around. I'm getting off." The driver wished her well when she exited. When I got off, he gave me plenty of time to plant my cane on the pavement before leaving the last step.

"Thanks so much," I said. What a contrast to the chunky Anglo driver I had ridden with who was stupid as well as surly. When activating his front-door, wheel-chair lift for a woman with a crippled child and two sibs, he ran it into a sign post which prevented full extension. Cursing and gasping, he tried several times, then bounced up and shook the apparatus. He was so mean that nobody pointed out the obvious solution. After more futile tries, and exclamations, he inched the bus forward permitting the lift to reach ground level.

As the woman pushed the wheel chair down the aisle with one hand and guided a child with the other, he goosed the bus—trying to make up for lost time. A Latino male bounced from his seat, ordered passengers off a bench seat parallel to the long side of the bus, lifted it, and secured the wheel chair in the niche he had created. He kept shouting at the driver who stopped the bus and strode to the wheel chair. "I take your number," the Latino shouted. "Don't start bus till chair ees fixed. Help this woman."

"That chair is her problem. You don't know the law. Don't give me no more trouble."

At my bus stop, the one-legged beggar was at the corner as usual, and several men, who were passing out leaflets, shouted angrily to the crowds in Spanish. To ease the pain in my leg I leaned against a building, carefully pressing the wallet in my left front pocket against the limestone to frustrate pickpockets. I gasped at an emaciated youth, with white hair falling to his waist, stumbling and weaving as he begged. There were raw cracks in his bare feet, and his eyes were sullen and desperate. I trembled when I read his placard: "I have AIDS." Had I not been afraid that my fat wallet would attract muggers, I would have given him a dollar immediately.

"Damn!" Pain stabbed my left leg as I started after the beggar, then stopped. Caution, not pain, kept me from helping him. To take my mind off his plight, I relived the most comical scene in three weeks of bus riding.

It all began when a large Anglo woman, sitting on seat C of the bench running parallel to the long side of the bus, made random remarks to nobody in particular. When she complained that the police didn't arrest a jay-walker, a jolly African American male, sitting in seat A of the same bench, chortled, "Maybe they want him get killed so dey don't have to bother with him no more." Cutting short other passengers' laughter, the woman turned toward him and talked non-stop about selective law enforcement, projected summer weather following the winter's El Nino, whether it was best to drive or take the bus, her allergies, Los Angeles vs. San Diego, the futility of speeding in city traffic since everyone had to wait for the next red light, the merits of large vs. small cars and buses vs. subways. While the stunned African American gaped and pretended to listen, an Oriental woman, who took seat B between them, adjusted politely to the situation by perching uncomfortably on the edge of her seat to allow the Anglo eye contact with her listener.

Then my leg started hurting and I had no place to lie or sit except the pavement—and I wasn't sure I could get back up without help. Anticipating another day at the hospital left me emotionally wretched. At least my son would be unconscious and pain free—incubated on an oxygen machine, sedated and anesthetized.

"Oh God, I'm so sorry he's going to die. And I can do nothing meaningful." How slowly time passed by his bedside. I held his hand till it warmed up, then took his other hand. I read the screen whose multi-colored lines described pulse rate, blood pressure and respiration. I identified short-term trends, made projections, and converted his temperature from centigrade to Fahrenheit by multiplying by 1.8 and adding 32. It's incredible how little time all this took.

The bus trip to the hospital started badly. After misjudging where the bus would stop, I was shoved to the end of the line and had to stand as the bus bucked forward. Then the driver said that we would be slowed by street repairs. And I alarmed the schizophrenic lady who always complained that people were staring at her. She grabbed my arm and screamed, "Get your eyes back in your own head."

Bus riding was still my preference. No taxis or rental cars! The schizo would get off at the third stop and I'd get a seat as the bus moved out of the downtown past the court house where O.J. Simpson was tried, and the purple Australian jacarandas straggling along the street. The electronic screen would soon stop flickering above my son, and I'd ride my last L.A. bus. From my son's apartment where I was staying, it cost about $40 to go to the airport by taxi if your driver took the best route, or you could pay $25 for a shuttle cab that made numerous detours to fill it to capacity. I'd walk a half block for a number 206 bus going West, transfer to the Metro Green Line Train, get off at Aviation Station and catch a free shuttle bus. My senior citizen's bus ticket would cost $.45 with a dime for the transfer.

Since I rode the number 71 bus which went to the top of the hill behind the hospital, unlike the number 70 which stopped at the bottom, I got seated beside a group of Anglos on crutches or carrying canes—all going to the outpatient clinic. During my weeks of bus riding, I'd gotten to know some of them and explained why, despite my cane, I wasn't going to the clinic.

"You're looking good today," a heavy man with a mustache said.

"You too," I said. He was so amiable that I had told him about my son's speech trophies, school and college plays, and the times we'd taken him to the theatre in Kansas City and New York where we saw Lauren Bacall. "Good to see you, Mark."

"How's your boy, the actor, doing?"

"Unconscious, no hope." My eyes began to water.

"Don't say that. There's great power in the human spirit. There's always hope."

"Not with AIDS, killer pneumonia, both lungs collapsed, blood pressure falling, kidneys failing." I wiped away tears with the back of my hand.

"How sad," a woman said. "You love your son very much."

"More than anyone, but don't tell my wife."

"How's she taking this?"

"She's touring Europe with friends and doesn't know I'm in L.A., that my son's terminal. She can't reach me at home in Missouri, and I don't answer my son's phone here. So she calls my sister who repeats my lie that some college friends persuaded me to take a trip through the Ozarks, that I can't be reached because they stop when they feel like it and camp out."

"Shouldn't she be coming to the hospital with you?"

"Not since my son's totally unconscious, and won't ever wake up."

"How sad. So you're alone with him all day?"

"No, his friends visit him. Some fly in from all over the country. Men and women he went to school with in Missouri, people who liked the poetry he read in coffee houses around L.A., friends he made as an actor in New York, Chicago and the West Coast."

"And people from work?"

"No," I said. "He's been unemployed for months. This week, a woman he knew in high school came in from Seattle. Two guys he graduated with at the University of Missouri flew from Memphis. Last week, two women came from Kansas City.

"Did they know he was unconscious before they came."

"Yes."

"It's wonderful those friends care so much," a woman said. "It must be comforting that so many people love your son."

"That depends," I said, choking. From surreptitiously reading his private journals a year ago, I knew that my son had been gay for 11 years and practiced random sex. Maybe he had been HIV positive for five years—nobody knew because he had refused to be tested. If so, and he had infected a partner each month, and these partners had done likewise creating ever-widening ripples of death, my son might have caused more misery than the Oklahoma City bombing. I didn't know enough math to figure it out.

"Sorry, I didn't mean to upset you before your long day."

"I'm OK. I keep busy in the hospital. Today, I brought some of my son's poetry to edit. He never could punctuate or spell. Maybe I'll try to get his work published." I unfolded some pages, and scanned the poem I had just corrected.

SENSELESS
(n.d.)

I finally figured out what it is I need.
I need a seeing-eye man—
     obedient, muscular, calm, cool and collected.
Oh Lord, send me a German shepherd.
Baaaaaa! Oh Lord, I can't see.

Senseless and Sensitivity

I won't put you in a harness—
    only hold my hand and help me cross the street.
Tell me when it is safe, guide me to the other side,
Show me my true reflection.
I need an ophthalmologist.
Make me wear coke bottle glasses.
I will abandon vanity if you will only make me see.

I am helpless in the world of vision.
I have been blinded by the glare of reality and taxes.
My sight has been clouded by airheads.
There was that nasty accident in the gym.
It is always fun until someone loses an eye.
Behind the glare there is darkness just as startling,
And I have to open my eyes as wide as they will go
To try to take it in—to try to comprehend the lights are on.
I know the lights are on.
I'm obsessive-compulsive; I checked.
The lights are on, but I'm sitting in this world of darkness.
I want infrared vision.
I want the words to describe the darkness.

Oh God, I am mute too.
I open the sphincter muscle of my mouth
As wide as it will go—the giant vortex of communication—,
And strain and force and pray.
I pray some word—any word—will fight its way up
From the prison of my inner being—
Up through the lungs and trachea—,
Claw through the dust and smoke and ashes—,
Attach itself to some motivated hunk of phlegm
And come spewing out into this waiting, wondering world,
And explain what it is I mean when I say that I am blind.
Can't you see I cannot see? I cannot function.
Where is my handicapped hang-tag
So I can park in the spaces right in front of the library?
Oh yeah, that's right, I DO NOT HAVE A CAR.
I will lie down in the handicapped parking space,
Wait to be run over, sue, win, buy a car or two.

And then you will give the hang-tags and the stickers,
And it will be recognized that I am senseless.

"I see you're better now," the woman said when the bus stopped at the rear of the hospital.

"Oh, sure. Thanks for your concern."

"There's one thing I wonder about. Would you mind if I asked you a question?"

"No. Go ahead."

"Well." Her voice quavered. "I got to say goodbye to my mom, but not my dad. I'm awful sorry about that. Before he went into coma, did you get to say goodbye to your son?"

"Goodbye was too discouraging," I said. "After he went to Intensive Care and lived on tubes all doped up, I read poetry to him when he was conscious. I said the family and all his friends were pulling for him, that he was a beautiful person and I was proud to have him for a son."

"That's nice. What did he say"

"He motioned for pen and paper, then wrote 'I'm very blessed.'"

"What a comfort. He found peace."

"And one more thing," I blurted. "Every day when I leave I kiss his cold forehead." I hid my head and sobbed, trying not to yell like the schizo. My nose dripped down my jacket and I had forgotten my Kleenex.

"I got to make the next run," the driver finally said. "You can get off now or ride for an hour till the bus gets back here. The passengers said your son's going to die. Sorry! I seen you coming here lots of times. You done all you could."

I waved thanks and wiped my nose on my sleeve. Then I limped to the front-door exit. "Horrible month," I whispered. It began with my biweekly phone call to ask about my son's job search and how much money to send. When he said he was down with "the flu that's going around," I urged him to visit a clinic, call a hotline or contact his social-worker friend about emergency services. As always, he ended the call with "I love you."

I didn't hire an ambulance or rush to L.A. When he said he was better the next day, I again suggested he get medical attention. When he later reported that the clinic had had no appointments, I asked him to keep seeking medical care and to contact me about any problem. But, too late to save him, the hospital phoned me.

Senseless and Sensitivity

II.

MELANCHOLIC VISIONS
(1968–1986)

Rob was born in Marietta, Ohio during that muggy July when we left for Gainesville, Florida where I joined the University of Florida's Social Sciences Department. His 11-year-old brother somehow cut his forehead badly after hearing about the birth—perhaps a bad omen foreshadowing that the two boys would never become pals. We paid too much attention to Rob without explaining to his elder that a baby has special needs.

From his earliest days, Rob rarely cried or balked at eating or sleeping. He didn't mind being confined in a play pen. He liked being attended to, but he seemed satisfied with watching what took place, and waiting for his turn without resentment or anger.

Without significant illness or trauma, he talked and walked—virtually always serene. He delighted in riding to a park, with or without a friend or two, where I pushed him on the swing.

He was soon fascinated by TV and ultimately began to imitate the actors. We placed him in an acting class for his peers before he entered school. Not far into his school years, he started talking about a movie career and buying a mansion in Hollywood. He didn't need structured activities or companions because he had his dreams and fantasies.

Rob was tall and blue-eyed with blondish-brown hair like me, while his brother was shorter, brown-eyed and dark haired like his mother. He loved swimming in our pool and having the neighborhood kids over each Sunday afternoon. Somehow he got some bleach and dyed patches of his hair whitish-blonde, then said that the pool water had caused the transformation. When a doctor raised a question about his hair, I jocularly repeated his story.

Nearly always happy, such thrills as peddling his new "Big Wheel" trike, going to the beaches on the Atlantic coast, or taking his chums to see the film version of "Grease" triggered his magic, soft smile that touched me deeply.

Without being aggressive about it, he craved and offered affection; but I fell short in responding because of my fear of spoiling the child and/or encouraging homosexuality. (I've read that such attitudes toward child-raising were common in the first third of the twentieth century when my parents acquired them and transmitted them to me.) But Rob's gentleness and affectation made him a favorite of our relatives and friends.

Contrary to my example of shrugging off every sort of disappointment as part of life—a trait of my Quaker forebears—, he was cruelly wounded by personal slights and rejection. When Rob was about seven, his brother left Florida by plane for the University of Chicago. Amid the hassle and tension at the airport, Rob kept pushing and tugging for his brother's attention, the burst into heart-rending sobbing when Mike pushed him away.

Ten years later, in Fayette, Missouri where I taught at the local college, he purchased a "Dungeons and Dragons" set, read the rules, fondled the pieces and girded up for combat. But some neighbor boys borrowed the set, took it to another home, and wouldn't let him play. Rob hid his feelings alone in his room that long winter afternoon.

Generally, he was popular—even adored—outside our family. He had close chums among boys his age in Gainesville. A neighbor lady mothered him passionately. A little girl could hardly wait to start kissing him and didn't want to stop. We joined the Methodist Church before we left Florida, and regularly attended services while I was at Central Methodist College in Fayette, Missouri. (I even taught Rob's Sunday School class for a time.)

In Fayette, a few tough kids shoved him about in the school hallways, but he never retaliated. He had some male chums in middle school, then became popular in high school. He had long talks with girls—sometimes at our home—, dated some girls and palled around with members of the speech-and-drama group.

Through his school years, crowned by becoming high school valedictorian, we didn't solve three problems that later affected Rob's life and poetry. When his Gainesville elementary school alerted us regarding his "feminine behavior," we decided to ignore the matter during his minority unless his happiness and success seemed threatened. And he did so well until his junior year of college that we felt vindicated. Since we believed that he had the right to choose his sexual practices when he reached adulthood, it didn't seem wise to explore this sensitive matter with him at age 20.

Medicating his acne lead to years of difficult discussions. I dropped a dermatologist for recommending accutane, which then had a list of adverse side effects. I was disgusted when the doctor said that he would prescribe corrective medicines if accutane produced blood pressure or triglyceride problems. Since Rob was doing so well, a smooth skin didn't seem worth the risks.

Based on my experiences with acute acne, I projected that Rob could be socially successful till the acne disappeared completely around age 35. Despite his pleas, I never allowed him take accutane while he was a minor. (With stern warnings, I helped him obtain a few doses later.) After Rob's acne improved in his late 20s, and accutane was found to be devastating to pregnant women and factor in higher suicide rates, I thought I had done the right thing. But acne-related damage to his self-esteem may have contributed to his self-destructive life style.

Coping with his straggling teeth and overbite failed. I chose an orthodontist who removed teeth to make room for others to form a uniform pattern under pressure from braces. Rob's mouth seemed to improve for years, but ultimately the braces didn't do the job. As for an orthodontist breaking his jaw and resetting it, I said that Rob could undertake that himself if he wished. Although his bite was imperfect, I thought him exceedingly handsome. Again, I was unwilling to jeopardize his soma for cosmetic purposes.

It worried me a bit when he got his ear pierced during high school and wore an ear ring at times. It seemed to be some sort of statement of independence or self-determination, like dying his hair, so I didn't protest.

We had several big surprises as Rob grew up. He was so completely disinterested in athletics that I soon abandoned pitching balls for him to hit, playing catch, etc. Croquet and swimming were his things, but he was too complacent to make them competitive sports. Though most boys enjoy running at any pretext—or none—I never saw him run till he was about nine years old.

At a large picnic in rural Florida, some 20 children—many of them older than Rob—took part in a race. He took long strides and steadily increased his lead over about 1/3 of a mile to win easily without breathing hard. And he wasn't pleased, just glad to be finished. I was amazed that he ran so well, but never suggested that he be timed, or start training. He jogged some in his 20s, but never ran competitively again.

I was repeatedly surprised by Rob's commitment to acting and his verbal ability. In all his speech contests, dramatic productions and rehearsals, I never heard him mispronounce a word. Every syllable sounded clearly in large gyms regardless of distractions.

When we moved to Missouri in 1978, it appeared that he would have to wait for a higher grade level to appear in a play. But he got a part in a college production of "Once Upon a Brute Beast" depicting Jake Troll—an elf (mischievous child). I drove him to the college for rehearsals and performances. He was nervous offstage, relaxed when the curtain rose.

In high school, he appeared in some three plays or shows each year. Besides taking him to see the "Go-Goes" in Kansas City, we heard Debbie Boone sing "You Light Up My Life" in Columbia and attended plays in several cities. (Seeing Kevin Kline in "Arms and the Man" and Lauren Bacall in "Woman of the Year" during New York trips may have influenced his wish to move to New York City after college.) One summer, I took an unfilled part to join with Rob in a community-theatre production of "Murder on the Nile." He sometimes paused for laughter that never came because the director had revised the text so extensively that his punch lines meant nothing to the audience. At least he enjoyed the cast party I gave after the final performance.

During his lifetime, we saw brief passages from the journals that he began during his junior year for English class. He apparently showed his songs and poems in the journal to friends to whom they were dedicated; but the only one we saw was the winner of the Columbia Art League's first prize. Hearing him read it at a League ceremony was an even bigger thrill than his graduation at which he received several awards, and we heard a good speech by Roger Wilson, the future governor of Missouri.

Reading the text of the journals revealed someone who was very excited about school, drama, popular music, girl friends, male chums and his future. Rob perfectly expressed the intensity of youth, his dismay because his favorite drama teacher left the high school, and a craving for life's adventures. Resuming his journal in the fall of 1985, he rhapsodized about his five-week stay at Northwestern University's theatre program for high school students.

In Alfred Jarry's "Ubi Roi," Rob played the female lead. (The director cast a female for the male lead in this absurdist comedy.) The children of three famous entertainment personalities were in the cast, which received standing ovations after each of its two performances. He was "very proud" of his performances. He fell in love with a girl from New York City and made many new friends. Leaving them proved "incredibly hard" and triggered considerable self discovery.

We stayed up all night the last night we had together and walked to Lake Michigan (2 blocks away) to see the sun rise. It was so beautiful!!

Leaving that morning was Hell!! Everyone was sobbing—including me. I am not much of one to cry but I broke down four times in those five weeks. I cried the last day of core classes—everyone cried. I cried at the final banquet—everyone cried (some wailed)....

I think it is important that I let myself cry this summer. Actors have to have a certain amount of vulnerability—no matter what character one is playing.

One of the most important things I learned this summer is that acting is not putting on a mask—it is taking a mask off. I think I've always agreed with that—I just didn't know how to say it.

It is hard to describe the magic that happened this summer. Words cannot express....

And he couldn't keep food on his stomach during the final day at Northwestern.

The initial explanation of his poetry dates from February, 1985 when he was disturbed about world-wide suffering and poverty. Writing poetry down after reflecting on images and ideas was a form of release from frustration. "If someone who read my poetry didn't know me, he might think I was insane or suicidal." But he had "too much living to do" to be suicidal. "What keeps me sane is my knowledge that there is life after Fayette."

He planned to enter "Ghost Town" and "Less Than Meets the Eye" in a poetry contest; if he did, he got no recognition.

The first poem expressed his view that so many Fayette people "are so inactive and so closed-minded that they might as well be dead." The second was a statement on originality that largely "seems to be extinct in this town." Since persons who were original in thought, dress or anything were shunned, Rob cited the aphorism "Be different and be damned."

Rob liked to write in black ink because it was "a delightfully morbid color," "so sexy and mysterious," and "no fashion sin was ever committed in black." Furthermore:

"Black also symbolizes death, I guess I have a slight obsession with death—not my own—just death in general. It is such a cool thing to write about. Most of the poems and stories I write have some sort of reference to death."

He said that he usually wrote about conditions around him, rather than about himself, but that exhaustion filled his mind with bizarre images like those expressed in "A Poem for Murderers, the Insane, and Other Teenagers." Sometimes, he claimed, "dreams (even nightmares) make more sense (or seem to make more sense) than reality."

"Realizations" is a reliving of his date with a girl who began the evening by saying that she didn't want to have a relationship. The poem describing a search for the girl who was "not there" grew from a walk through the Columbia Mall hoping by chance to see his friend—probably the Columbia girl he had met at Northwestern. (Because he wasn't writing for publication, left many of his poems and songs untitled.) Rob wrote the poem about conversations with a stranger after a visit to a friend in college. (The two had drifted apart.)

Hoping to become a songwriter for "a totally cool band," Rob included his song lyrics in several journals—calling his inability to write music a "technicality." His male English teacher, who had written so many supportive and witty comments in prior journals, said that he should sing the songs in person or turn in a cassette of the music.

Rob's poem about a shattered love was inspired by meeting a college girl he admired greatly but never dated. In a strange twisting of poetic license, he wanted the phrase, "Following my heart," to be taken literally. "I want the heart to be physically gone and I want the narrator to actually follow it."

The poem about jealousy was triggered by seeing a girl he broken up with at the end of his junior year dating another boy. He thought the piece had a "flow problem" and was frustrated with it. "God, I hate rhymes! I've been experimenting with them lately and if they aren't extremely clever, which mine seldom are, they sound so trite." (He wrote two more poems about this girl during December, 1985.)

Rob sought his teacher's advice about punctuation to ensure that his poems would be read as he intended. Complaining that he fell easily into verbal excess while writing, Rob strove for "realism"—discussing the "most complex emotions using the simplest words." While writing his May 4, 1986 journal entry when he had little to report, he received phone notification that his "Faye Morrison" had won a first place award from the Columbia Art League. He then expressed his emotions (implicitly thanks) to his teacher "to get the excitement of the moment in writing."

Several poems at the end of this section express how keenly Rob was disturbed by such major changes in his life as ending old activities, striking the set after a play was over, leaving familiar settings, and separating from friends. He wrote about the transition from high school to college as follows:

> I will always remember the summer I turned 18 as the summer I cried. And cried. And cried. I can't believe that people are leaving and that I'm growing up....
>
> I know that ___ will always be a friend, but distance and time will change us both—and "it" will never be the same....
>
> One minute I'm bursting with excitement, the next minute I'm sobbing buckets! I want to go on with my life, but it is hard to break the ties. And yet I don't want to break the ties. I just don't want them to become nooses!! It is all so difficult.

A critical reader might well ask why it would be hard to leave Fayette after all the harsh things he had written about the town's stifling of originality. The journal shows, however, that Rob's attitudes and moods were transitory and frequently inconsistent. For instance, he finally concluded that Fayette was a great place to develop originality. Sometimes he said he could confide only in girls; then he describes "good talks" with boys—even one with me.

There is a vast inconsistency between the life affirmation of his journal text and his poems and songs during high school. Life was fun, he wrote. He wanted to become an actor, start a band called the "Vicious Circles," help other people as a teacher or psychologist, devote his fortune—presumably acquired through movie stardom—to the needy and the homeless, and work for world peace and justice by founding "Actors Against Annihilation" which would uplift the masses by free performances.

The poems and songs, however, are often lurid depictions of the dark side of life (fascination with death, broken relationships, rejection, cruelty and futility) in quasi-surreal, occult settings. Hence Section I is called "Melancholic Visions." Like most of the sections, it ends with wrenching farewells, agonizing personal reassessments, and moving on to another place or to death's disintegration.

16 Senseless and Sensitivity

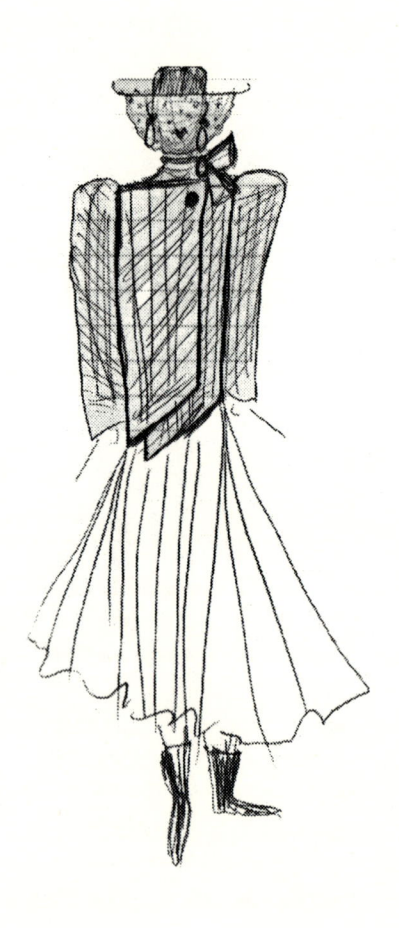

GHOST TOWN

Walking to the graveyard,
Living cadavers in our dated block
Sneer at me.

I live with dead people.
I watch the living die
As they drown in unfulfilled dreams and stale coffee.

The marble is cold and calm;
The giant oak breathes life.
He has fulfilled the promise of the seed.
The marble quietly shades the dead
Who have been dead longer than they have been buried.

I return to the city of ideal death
And think of all the anxious marble
Waiting for corpses to finish dying.

LESS THAN MEETS THE EYE

In a plexiglass nightclub
In the long-forgotten future,
Blue-eyed, blonde-haired plastic people
Sway uniformly
To synthetic-cliche dronings:
"Drone—I love you, doo wah, I love you—Drone."

The uniform movements become faster
And the happy plastic people merge
To form the perfect human being.

The PERFECT human being!

The perfect human being
Slithers gracefully to the streets
And engulfs everything in its path.

(n.t. 2/28/85)

They sit in the den of sin
Watching the people stroll by.
Memories stir.
Didn't 25 used to be 5?
The barkeep loses track
Of the number of drinks
They have drunk.
He knows they won't pay.
They can't.
They wonder if
This is their 10th
Or their 15th.
They can't remember,
But they don't care.
It all has the same effect—
Whether it's the 10th
Or the 15th
It all kills the pain
Of living through death.
Or is it dying because of life?

IN NOVEMBER

In November
Their white hair is
Covered with pastel scarves—
Faded and worn with age
(Like their wearers).
He smiles shyly.
They know him from their past.
He will forget them in his future.

In November
Their raspy voices
Scratch in the back of his mind.
Their hands, bird talons,
Claw his shoulder.

"What a handsome boy,"
They cackle.
He shudders and cries.

In November
The cold wears them down.
They rake the leaves
That cover their little yards
For the last time.
Soon the leaves cover them.
Serene marble looms over them.
Every day becomes November.

ODE TO ME: PART I

Morning light comes.
What will I do with my life?
Lie to me bathroom mirror!
Oh! You little tramp!
You contort my features
For your pleasure.
Who am I kidding
As I throw up
In the bathroom sink?

Thrown together,
We (aren't we majestic)
Proceed to the
Pit of knowledge.
Teach me! Teach me!
I dare you!

Inflict me with knowledge.
I live for pain.
Go ahead—make my day.

At home, by candlelight,
I write my lessons
On an old paper bag

With a piece of coal.
Study, Study!!!
It will get you out of the gutter.
Where will it take you?
To another gutter
Where the people think
They have more class.

Oh, no! The candle is gone!
The homework will have to wait till tomorrow.
Yes, Scarlett, even though frankly, my dear,
I don't give a damn,
Tomorrow is another day.

A POEM FOR MURDERERS, THE INSANE, AND OTHER TEENAGERS

I lie on the floor.
A vulgar light shines in my pupils.
I am dead (or feigning that state);
Morbid thoughts twist through my head.
I contemplate suicide;
But I'm already dead, I think.

The ceiling turns into a sea
Of shocking red blood.
I feel it in my heart and on my hands.
I taste it in my mouth.
What a pleasant flavor—bittersweet.
The original sin crashes around me
And I am engulfed.

I awake from my nightmare of reality.
A white plaster ceiling stares at me—
No blood. A sacrificial dagger,
Warm in my palm, whispers the truth.
My real world is gone.
I enter the insanity of a sunny day.

(n.t. 3/24/85)

I am not suicidal.
I am not suicidal.
I want to live
But not like this.
I am scared of invisible things
That scratch my back ever so lightly
With blood-red fingernails.
They are not there, and yet they are.
Their pressure eats at my existence

I hurt. Oh God, how I hurt.
The only way to stop the hurt
Is to hurt someone else.
This would be breaking a promise.

It's such a vicious circle.
Everything is such a vicious circle.
No—it couldn't be a vicious square.
It had to be a vicious circle.

Around and around and
Around and around and around,
Eating, gnawing, smothering.

This is not a poem.
I am not suicidal.
I am not suicidal.
I love life.
This is not a poem.
This is my cardboard existence.

(n.t. 4/23/85)

The lights of the town
That I see from the hilltop
Twinkle and whisper
Too many secrets of too many people:
Screams of dead babies,

Screams from battered wives,
Screams from broken fathers.
All this and more
Comes from one little house
In one little town
Under the big black sky.

REALIZATIONS

She looked out the car window
And didn't say anything
For a very long time.
She remembered dancing
In a different world
With another boy.

As the trees and the night flew by,
They each counted their faux pas
And reflected on the evening.

He drummed his fingers
On the steering wheel and realized
That it isn't the real thing every time.
Yet, as she walked away, he knew
There were possibilities in long hair.

LET'S NOT SHOUT

It's one o'clock at night,
'bout time to start another fight.
Round one's just begun;
This isn't going to be fun

Let's not shout.
We'll wake the neighbors.
Don't shout!
They're probably in bed.
Let's not shout.
We'll wake the neighbors.

Don't shout!
Our yells could raise the dead.

The fight is halfway through;
The clock has just struck two.
We're in such a fix.
I have to get up at six.

Let's not shout.
I'm too tired to yell.
Don't shout!
It isn't worth the pain.
Let's not shout.
I'm too tired to yell.
Don't shout!
Why can't you refrain?

You stormed out the door.
You couldn't scream anymore.
The fight is over and done,
But nobody has won.

Let's not shout.
What's the reason?
Don't shout!
What's it all about?
Let's not shout.
What's the reason?
Don't shout!
Let's try to work things out.

(n.t. 10/6/85)

Child abuse is such a pretty thing
When dime-store claws
Slap dirty little faces in front yards
Littered with broken toys.

Baby was just imitating the way
Daddy hit mommy in the sweaty bedroom
Amid muffled screams.

(n.t. 10/6/85)

The me of yesterday
And the day before
Are behind the mirror—
Frozen in glass—suspended in time.

I move in circles—tossed by waves.
I'm always questioning how my heart behaves.
As each day brings new recollections
I search the mirror for my reflection.

(n.t. 10/6/85)

In the crowded room behind reality
I look for you every time I see
The bleached blonde hair that you wear.
The girl turns around and you're not there.

In the dark I search and hope to find
The only person who can ease my mind.
My shattered heart is suspended in air.
The girl turns around and you're not there.

The silhouette acts so strange.
It looks like yours—unless you've changed.
If I find you, what would I say?
I guess it doesn't matter anyway.

I walk out fast but turn to see
If you're back there staring through me.
I know you're near me floating through the air.
I turn around and you're not there.

MOTTO #1

Years from now, as we search our hearts,
We will wonder where the missing pieces went.
And we will recall the tears shed
And the laughter shared.
And we will remember
Giving part of ourselves to each other.
And we will realize that
We would do it all again.

MOTTO #2

As we travel our separate paths
We must remember that all roads lead home,
And that as soon as we reach into our pockets
We will find memories, dreams, laughter, and tears.
And no matter how greatly our paths diverge,
Part of us will always remain here as one.

(n.t. 10/24/85)

Tripping over red,
    Morning,
Like a football player,
Tackles me to my senses.

Staggering into blue,
    Night,
Like a drunken hooker,
Drags me back to a world
Of forgotten people

And old blue-jean faded memories

(n.t. 10/24/85)

Conversations pass like ships in the night
As I sit with a stranger
I have known too many years.

SONG #1

You ask if I love you.
What a cliche!
I don't have to answer;
I prove my love to you every day.
You hate the mornings.
I have to fight you from your dreams.
Life would be easier if you realized
Things aren't always what they seem.

Chorus:

I'll walk the line for you
And when the day is through,
You'll know my love is true
'cause I walk the line for you.
And if the mirror
Doesn't show you what you want to see,
You know you can turn to me
And I'll be what you want me to be.
I'll walk the line for you
And when the day is through,
You'll know my love is true
'Cause I walk the line for you.

Thoughts of old lovers
Bring back old fears.
When the fears overcome you,
I'll be the one to hold you near.
The shadows taunt you
As they crawl across our wall.
You know I'll pick up the pieces
If you ever take a fall.

(Chorus)

You won't think about tomorrow;
You say it makes you weak.
You say the hope for the future

Is too dark and bleak.
If we discover
Love isn't what we're looking for
We can let go lightly
As we calmly shut that door.

        (n.t. 10/25/85)

I crossed the sea
And followed you into your house.
And decided to stay a while.
The sun rose and set
And the moon waked and waned
Many times before our day was done.

As we knew would happen,
The homemade promises
Precariously balanced on burdened shelves,
Began to fall and shatter like saucers.

Lies couldn't mend what glue couldn't mend.
So we swept the shards out the kitchen door
And decided to watch another rerun.

Following my heart, I left
In search of another house
On the darker side of the horizon.

        (n.t. 10/31/85)

The only things that separate us
Are islands of furniture and confusion.
Across the sea of envious green
I see your foreign eyes jump to conclusions.

I know your looks aren't what they seem.
I find reality only in my dreams.
I said I didn't want to play the game;
But when you're with him
My feelings aren't the same.

Daggers pierce my heart
As your ship drifts out to sea.
A glance in the mirror confirms

That your cargo is a piece of me.
The sun sets over the waves;
The moon rises over the beach.
I search for something I've discarded.
I grope for something out of reach.

SEASONS AND REASONS OF THE ONE THING FOR WHICH WE ALL LIVE AND DIE

The magnets pull me
Between either pole.
I don't know why
I feel so old.

When I look at the world
Through your rose colored glasses,
I see all the things
You saw pass us.

I don't know why
Our love died in the Spring.
I don't know why
Things aren't what they seem.

Now my heart is in eternal Winter—
A fruitless, barren season.
I search this vacuum
For a reason.

I wish I could give you
A map of what you're looking for.
I'd frame it
In the gold of yore.

I'd bronze it with
The kiss of tomorrow
If I only thought
I would end the sorrow.

I contemplate the patterns
On the kitchen wall.
And plan ways to rescue you
From our Fall.

GHOSTS

Like a voice from the grave,
Your face hurls me back to reality.
Your glares pierce my vulnerable heart of steel.
Your stares remind me of forgotten days.

From the sepulcher of my heart
You rise to challenge my sanity.
I feel your touch though you're not near.
I reel in pain from invisible hands.

If I ever bury you,
I will be gone for good
To rooms of padded satin,
To tombs of lipstick-stained corpses.

ODE TO ME: PART II

I have only ONE question for you:
Would you still love me if I had magenta eyebrows?
Freud would be so shocked if he knew
What I was thinking.

Did you know I had another bout of drinking?

Diet cokes don't help me sleep.
I have to face the night.
Sleeping pills won't set things right.

The writing on the walls of morning
Comes too soon.
And then come facts to face:
I'm on point; my hair is flat.
I'm out of mousse—What's the use?
I feel fat.
So I eat another chocolate doughnut.
The car won't start. I broke my heart.
All this before I left the driveway.
I finished picking up my friends
Only to find I don't have time
To pick up myself.
Oh well—I guess I'll be late.

There goes the sun
To brighten a stranger's day.
I hope HE likes getting out of bed.
Should I tell him what's going to happen?

No, I'll let him read the book.

SONG #2 ("And I Wait")

I'm patiently washing the dishes
From the dinner we had last night.
Is it wrong or is it right
To wish you were here?
I know you're driving straight into the dark.
You're hitting green lights; I see red!
I tumble and toss and fall into bed.
I am vacant; I rave and rant.
What's the use 'cause you can't hear me?
What's the use 'cause you're not near me?

Chorus:

It's not the fear of falling;
It's the fear of being alone.
Is that the phone?

God! I hope you're calling.
It's the wrong number again and again.
It's the beginning and the end.
All in one moment, all in one tear,

I risk drowning alone in my bedroom.
And I wait, and I wait for you.

You left your clock in the bedroom.
It ticks like your heart; I fall apart
In front of the mirror you gave me
So I could see myself.
I keep it hidden on the shelf
In a box labeled with your writing:
"To save for a rainy day."
I know there's no way
That you're coming back.
The reason is you're above me.
The reason is you don't love me.

    (Chorus)

You picked me up just to see me fall.
I walk through the echoes in our hall.
The shadows trick me—
I think you're home.
But the door is blocked
And my heart is locked.
Strangers come and strangers leave.
They never get what you received.
My touch is warm; my eyes are cold.
My face is young; my heart is old.
I try so hard but I cannot feel.
I try so hard but it's not real.

    (Chorus)

SONG # 3 ("Blue Love")

Bring it home in a suitcase;
Hide it on the shelf.
When visitors drops in,
Be a mirror of normality.
Arrange the furniture
So everything seems regular.
Save it for the bedroom
Save it for the fantasies.

Chorus:

You're unreachable; I'm untouchable.
It's so unbelievable; it's so unnatural.
It's just a kiss away; it's just a touch away.
Save it for another day—
Blue love.

Messages through paper walls,
Cautious glances across the room.
Soon doesn't come fast enough.
Where are all the onlookers from?
When will they leave?
Lies are found out easily
When no one knows the truth.
Keep the faith to yourself.

(Chorus)

It's so hard on your mother.
Catholic grief pours out
In the bedroom where it all started.
Get back to the basics;
Burn the suburbs to the ground.
Righteousness will prevail
When all the freedom is gone.
So get your kicks while you can.

(Chorus)

We dig our own graves
With this love:
A hollow tombstone covered
With society's frown.
Blue tears are shed
Only in private.
A countenance of disgust
Is worn while strangers sneer.

(Chorus)

SONG #4 ("The River")

There is mud of the river
On your shoes.
Your nights are spent
In the blue-lit rooms.
If it was another lover,
I could understand.
Dancing lights are in your eyes
As you wait for the river.

Chorus:

You're so far under the river
I can't save you.
You're so far under the river
I can't see you.
You're so near me,
But your hands can't reach.
Your fingers trickle away
To the bottom of the river.

The bedroom is like chipped ice
Waiting for the river.
I feel you toss and turn.
Anxious hands don't know what to do
When they are empty.

You wish I was made of cool glass
So you could fill me with your love.
But I am fresh and much too warm.

        (Chorus)

In your eyes I see
Water from the river.
There's an empty bottle
Behind every broken heart.
Every motion is one of intoxication.
Every emotion is one of desperation.

        (Chorus)

FAYE MORRISON—1986 *

Faye Morrison
Looks in the glass,
Piles her hair on top of her head,
And calmly acknowledges the grey.

Locking her door behind her,
She trudges to town
Avoiding the fallen leaves
Raked into piles by younger generations.

Returning home,
No one offers to help her cross the street.
She collapses into herself,
And watches her heart roll into a corner.

Evening comes when the eyelids set.
Faye Morrison
Crawls under a patchwork quilt of rooftops,
And resumes her incestuous relationship with the American Dream.

*First prize in a high school competition sponsored
by the art league of Columbia, MO.

TODAY: A STUDY IN ORANGE

Black and white people, running hither and thither
Like chicken heads with their bodies cut off,
Spoke today of the GREAT TRAGEDY.

(I kept changing the station,
But I heard the same song.
We know all the answers,
But we still get everything wrong).

The truth hurts when our Gloucester eyes
Are yanked out of our heads
And forced to look at
What we don't want to see.

(Wish them away as hard as we might,
We can't hide the monsters in our closets
And pretend they're not there.)

The masses are sent to war
By those who "know best" as calmly
As a five-year old is sent to boarding school.
The soldiers are the only ones
Who really stay home.

Wisps-of-smoke people
Drift upwards to Heaven.
A secular few stoke the fire
And laugh at the flames.

(I wonder where all the ashes come from
As they mar the green perfection
Of my guilty front yard.)

DANCE OF LONELY FRIDAYS

Wrapped around a lonely Friday,
Your bridges burnt behind you,

The match is still in your hand
And your fingers feel very hot.

I want to reach out to you,
But I fear what your eyes would say.
When you flip the switch, the lights go off
And I cannot see.
This is the state you want me in.

You take the cold walk—eyes always facing forward.
Have you ever looked back at your heart and soul?
Dark demons dance in your empty rooms.
I see all this through your windows.

BLUE LADY

You're the color of indifference;
You're tomorrow's yesterday.
You don't want to reach out for the answers.
You just want to drift away.
You've got the smile of a statue:
Lips upturned, carved into stone.
I want to give you everything;
You just want to be alone.

Chorus:

Oh, blue lady!
Why do you have to be so blue?
Oh, blue lady!
How can I get through to you?

You run through the daylight,
So your thoughts won't catch up with you.
Always looking for a hiding place,
Maybe that's why you're so blue.
You unplug your answering machine
So you can answer the phone yourself.

You calmly tell me you're not home. Click!
And then I hear the dial tone start to melt.

(Chorus)

I can see you melting into bed.
Flowing with your programmed dreams,
You wash away into tomorrow
Just like Ophelia in the stream.
You are Sleeping Beauty carved in ice.
I want to touch you with my warmth,
But cold to hot often shatters.
This I know to be the truth.

(Chorus)

I want to tear down your walls
And see all your flaws—
Put a stone through your perfection.
I want to get on my knees
And see what you see—
Not some damn reflection.

(Chorus)

You're the color of indifference:
Cold, blue oozing into black.
You smile at me like I'm the perfect stranger,
But only when I've turned my back.
You walk away into forever;
You're just a shadow in my past.
I no longer want to hold you
'Cause I know it wouldn't last.

(Chorus)

A HINT OF STRANGENESS

Practicing to be an enigma, I drove by
Hoping that you would see me drive by,
Hoping that you would see me
Stare straight ahead.
I want to keep you guessing.
I want to keep you wondering.
But you were nowhere to be found.

FOOTPRINTS

I return to my starting point
For the millionth time.
I see, as I knew I would,
The footprints from the previous journey.
My travels have been long
And the footprints are filling with time—
Becoming hints, traces, shimmering memories.
They are destined to disappear
Unless I take the walk again.

A MILLION MILES AWAY
(For all the people I've left behind)

Oh, the world keeps on spinning
When the sun rises.
It's just my perspective that has changed.
Oh, the world keeps on spinning
Even though I've walked on past.
It's just my mind that's been rearranged.

Oh, I woke up to discover I'm a million miles away.
I don't know how I got here
Or how I can get back to you.
'Cause I'm a million miles away.
'Cause I'm a million miles away.

Oh, the colors of yesterday are still brilliant
Though they're seen through someone else's eager eyes.
Oh, the colors of yesterday no longer frighten me away
'Cause now I can see past all their wicked lies.

Oh, my vision is so much better now
That I'm a million miles away.
I don't know how I got here
Or how I can get back to you.
'Cause I'm a million miles away.
'Cause I'm a million miles away.

Oh, the people I've left behind don't even miss me
Because the me I've left for them is so deceiving.
Oh, the people I've left behind
Keep dreaming the same dreams each night
And the people I've left behind keep on believing.

They don't know I'm a million miles away.
I don't know how I got here
Or how I can get back to you.
'Cause I'm a million miles away.
I don't know how I got here
Or if I can get back to you.
'Cause I'm a million miles away.
'Cause I'm a million miles away.

KISSING FRIENDS GOODBYE
(Summer, 1986)

We never thought the mirror
Wouldn't show us what we wanted to see.
We never thought we'd have to see ourselves
In the light of someone else's reality.
And you never thought I'd walk on by
Without even stopping to say, "Hello."
And you never thought you wouldn't care
When I walked on by.

Chorus:

I've spent all my summer kissing friends goodbye.
In the silence of the kiss I know what I'll miss.
In the silence of goodbye we know the reason why
I've spent all my summer kissing friends goodbye.

I never thought that I could feel so old.
I never thought I'd stop believing all the lies we told.
And I never thought you'd walk on by
Without even stopping to say, "Hello."
And I never thought I wouldn't care
When you walked on by.

(Chorus)

It's funny to know that people think we've grown apart.
It's funny to know that our love is stronger than at the start.
And I guess I always knew we'd walk on by
While silently saying "Hello."
And I guess I always knew we'd smile inside
As we walked on by.

(Chorus)

ALL THIS SUMMER
(1986)

Why do you look to me for decisions
That I can't even make for myself?
Demons attack from the darker side
And I can't even fight back.

Oh, those shadows become people,
But people always seem to leave.
Alone I face the errors of my ways
And the days that come too soon.

Chorus:

All this summer I'll be mad.
I'm calmly waiting for the train.
Baby, I'm going to go insane.
All this summer I'll be mad.

I've found that I'm really invisible.
Conversations and smoke drift through me.
I walk cautiously through all the people
And wait for the mines to explode.

Oh, the voices become louder—
Even though all the people have left.
Alone I wait to be completely erased.
I can't face the mirror in me.

(Chorus)

I've decided I'm wise beyond my years.
Sanity has always eluded me.
I think I have all the answers.
It's accepting them that's hard.

Oh, I think I'll always be haunted
By people who have walked on by.
Alone I rebuild my fantasies
And wait for the strangers to come home.

THE TRAVELER

Yesterday,
The world wanted to put me under glass
And watch me writhe and squirm.
Everyone wanted to see my mediocre days fly by
And make them into what they weren't.

Today,
I've discovered that I've moved a million miles
From that place where I never really was.

                              Tomorrow,
I'll wake up and realize
That I'm not supposed to stay here either.

ODE TO A WISTERIA-DRAPED VERANDA

Tonight, for lack of better apparel
I decided to wear the air—
A decidedly heavy, Southern costume.
And since Scarlett O'Hara was nowhere to be found.
I poured mint juleps all over my body,
And mourned the fact that,
Frankly my dear, NOBODY gives a damn.

HOPES FOR A FUTURE CIVILIZATION

I hope when our civilization is dug up
And put under glass,
And examined, reexamined, and re-reexamined,
That THEY will laugh
At our bones and the remains of our guns,
And say, "Serves them right."

I hope THEY know
That the barren planet on which THEY reside
Was once EARTH,
And that there were trees and hills.
I hope THEY know
That there were greens, and blues, and yellows—
Not just the red we left behind.

I hope THEY will try to see
Our justification or our motivation
Behind death and destruction.
I hope THEY will try to see
That we killed for some elusive idea in which we believed.
I hope THEY find a dictionary
With a long definition of "freedom."

I hope THEY will try to see
That we murdered for something we thought was right.

I hope THEY know we were wrong.

THE MOVE

Today I was assaulted by reality.
I now look like the sprayed remains
Of a Kamikaze bug on a car windshield.
(That one, damn bug corpse that obscures perfect vision!)
I put on my sunglasses and watched forever end.

As I drift into another indefinite forever,
I wait for someone to hand me a box marked SANITY.
I suppose that would be too convenient.
I wouldn't want life to become a 7-11, Would I?

I think I'm ready to hang my skeletons in a new closet.
I keep reassuring myself that
I took out the garbage,
Turned off the oven,
Organized and categorized all my emotions perfectly,
Unplugged the iron,
And locked the back door.
I want the house to be ready for a new visitor.

NON-CATHOLIC GUILT

Dead possums ooze on the road.
Why do I feel as though I killed them all?

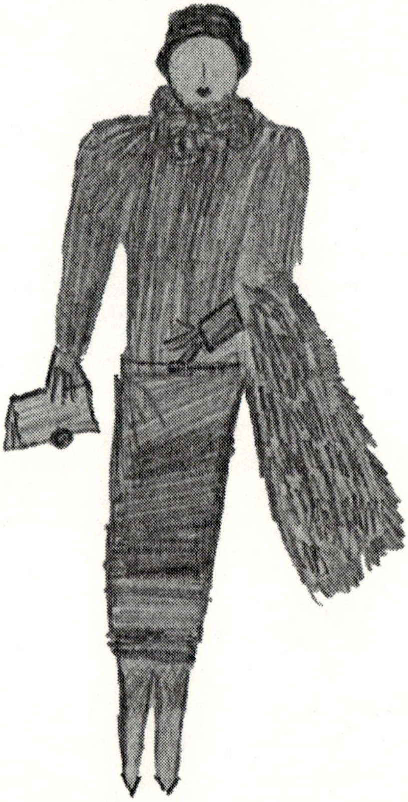

III.

COLLEGE YEARS: RATIONAL OBSERVATIONS: ACCEPTANCE OF GAY LIFESTYLE

Rob's journal is sporadic and brief for his four years at the University of Missouri—Columbia. Since we moved from Fayette to Columbia in May, 1987, and had a close relationship with Rob, I can give a first-hand account of many of his activities. After spending the 1986–1987 academic year in a dorm, he lived with us during his sophomore year. Then he spent two years in a shared apartment close to the campus.

As he had feared, many of his high school friendships broke down quickly. His best male chum treated him coldly at best during a visit to Kansas City. At his first high school homecoming after graduating, he felt he didn't belong. So he spent time with us that evening rather than joining his fellows at the abandoned railroad tracks for camaraderie and dissipation.

At first, he maintained his pattern of being "in love" with several girls simultaneously. One was "absolutely adorable" and seemed "pretty nice;" a second was "amazing;" and a theatre major was "cute." "She has a boyfriend, but Hell I am going to ask her out anyway." One clue to his changing sexual preference is that his poem-dedications began to name males. In a journal entry (January, 1988) he vented his lust for a male friend, then said, "I am gay...That is the first time I ever put that statement in writing…_____ thinks homosexual is such a clinical term. He prefers 'gay.'"

At the end of his freshman year, a dedicated poem explored his lifelong tendency to change lovers frequently:

> I could search these streets
> Forever and never find you.
> You've been swept away
> To cleaner places.
> Yes, I have this feeling
> I will never find you again.
> I doubt I'll even find a
> Reasonable facsimile.
>
> Yet I will keep on looking.
> And I honestly pray that you found
> What you desired—or returned
> To what you had.
>
> I will never forget that
> I had you trapped. Never
> Forget that I let you go.
>
> Please wake up hung over
> and remember my name
> and that you called me friend.
>
> I love you. I fall
> In love too easily.

This longing for a lover he let go is a repeat of his high school relationship with a girl. With high impulse levels and the tendency to "fall in love too easily," Rob's relationships were unstable for the rest of his life. Increasingly, he would be the partner suffering rejection.

His positive attitude toward academics was destroyed as completely as his heterosexuality. He started out in the "Honors College" and continued to excel. When he came home for Christmas after the first semester, he was impatient for his grades to arrive by mail. "I want a 4.0," he said repeatedly. "I want a 4.0 so much." And he danced about when he got the good news.

We were very pleased when he received notice that he was being considered for Phi Beta Kappa in his junior year. He soon faltered, however, and failed several courses plus incurring a $1,300 fine for late books, etc. In fact, he didn't graduate in May 1990 with his class, and had to take courses that summer to complete his degree.

Along with suggesting counseling, which he rejected, we tried and tried to find out what went wrong; but he revealed nothing. Again, we respected his privacy. Even years later, he would only say that he had become burned out. During this troubled period, we knew that he drank too much and smoked cigarettes. I tried to make the case against smoking many times. Neither the generality that over 300,000 Americans died each year from tobacco-related disease nor the specific tragedy of actor Yul Brenner's death from lung cancer made the slightest impression.

It proved too hard to reform a 20-year-old who had been so successful. We didn't want to force an open rupture since we enjoyed having him visit us so much. I recognized his problem of self-esteem and spent $100 to have his baby shoes bronzed when he noticed that mine and his brother's had been. I suspected that he was gay, although he did not confirm this for some four more years, and didn't want him to face this problem without general parental support. Besides, his acting and drama-related activities held up very well. It was such a pleasure to see him perform at the University and, occasionally, at local night clubs. We trusted that this passion would see him through this troubled period.

Not getting cast in any plays during his first semester reduced him to a form of depression, "a very black period." (He desperately missed "escaping into a character" and "the emotional contact with an audience." "There is nothing like feeling emotionally drained after an intense performance.") But he congratulated those who won parts and helped with sets and costumes. His first break was being cast in one-act plays staged by a class on directing. During his last three years he acted frequently in the student-run theatre called "Corner Playhouse" and in main stage productions directed by the faculty.

During the summer after his freshman year, Rob sketched original, female clothing designs for long hours. As he smiled and glowed while sketching, I came to believe that he would find some occupation in the drama world—even if it was costume design—, that he had sufficient commitment to make something happen.

We saved news photos of him acting, and a full-size likeness that stood in the theatre lobby during his performance in "Six Characters in Search of An Author." He played one female role; but his most memorable performance was Rich in "As Is," depicting the heart-rending despair of an AIDS victim. A news review said that he "makes the character so alive that his dying is a great tragedy."

Never being cast for the summer repertory theatre was perhaps the deepest hurt of his university drama career. (We rationalized that the faculty were looking for actors who had the musical talent required for many of their popular productions while Rob was a "serious" actor.) My vote for his finest achievement was being elected president of the Corner Playhouse, run by the drama students, for both his junior and senior years. He had to work well with upper classmen and graduate students, and do virtually everything that an entrepreneur has to do to make a theatre successful-even working during vacation breaks. (I considered the activity to be excellent management training.)

Rob had definite plans. In high school, he had recognized that acting was an "impractical" way to support oneself and considered getting certified to teach drama. We had several formal conferences with him about a "meal-ticket" degree or at least a supplementary program, such as computer courses or certification, to enhance his marketability. He insisted on completing his theatre-performance degree without any "meal-ticket" features.

For some unknown reason, he had decided against moving to New York and chose to go to Chicago. Given his partying, academic collapse and lack of employment goals besides acting, this wasn't promising. But the alternative of leaving him straining in Columbia without money or a job looked futile. He said that he would look for a job and try to break into the theatre in Chicago. (His single-minded acting success in Fayette and the university suggested that he deserved a shot while he had high hopes.) After he made one trip to Chicago and located an apartment, we bankrolled him with $8,500 and secured a van for him to drive. (HE SOLEMNLY PROMISED TO SEE A DOCTOR IF HE EVER BECAME ILL.)

His departure on August 11 was surely traumatic. He got up at 5:00 a.m. (about when he usually went to bed), was "nervous and queasy" at breakfast, then saw "my mother in the rear view of the Ryder truck leaning against my dad crying as I drove away." Then he hit a car on a Chicago street.

Some of Rob's college poems have the same melancholy that characterized his high school pieces. (But what's the difference between a high school senior and college freshman?) The bulk of them, however, are either love poems or rationalistic, detached accounts of occurrences. Several were written for a poetry class. He made two attempts to express his relationship with Mike, his elder brother, and relived learning to swim in Gainesville and leaving his grandmother's home in Waco, Texas a decade earlier.

Two poems toward the end of the section are very revealing. "Tuckerton After Meeting" is based on a photo (c. 1944). My bother and sister (Kirk and

Ellen), my mother, and I visited Quaker relatives at their summer home in Tuckerton each year. Rob's recognition that I looked "just like" him doubtless contributed to our love since I had long noticed the resemblance.

His untitled statement of preferences said that he hated work and living at home—attitudes that played key roles in his short, tragic life. He hated the feeling that he had to makes all A's, which helps explain his rebellion against academic excellence. Regrettably, he didn't do enough later on to ward off two other "hates": debt and AIDS.

POSITIVES

I saw a little boy walking down the street with his father—
Not an uncommon occurrence in the liberated '80s.
The little boy was counting:
"One, Two, Three, Four, Five, Six, Seven, Eight, Nine,
Ten, Eleven, Twelve, Thirteen, Fourteen...."

"Fifteen," said his liberated father. "Fifteen."
He sounded so confident, definite, final.
I wanted to run to him and explain the mysteries of
Imaginary numbers, fractions, decimals,
Square roots, and negative numbers;
But the sun was shining through the rain,
And I didn't feel like tampering with destiny.

DEATH NO. 5
(AN ENVELOPING, ENTICING PERFUME)

Today the world smells like Death—
Not that I have ever smelled Death—,
But when I do, I will recognize
That musty odor of ancient beach towels,
And I will say, "That is Death."

Besides the glorious odor of Death that chews us up,
But doesn't swallow;
There is rain on this Monday-Thursday.
(I didn't want to get out of bed.)
Perhaps we should view rain as a second baptism
(or a first or a hundredth);
But we, as vulnerable human beings, cower
Beneath our umbrellas.
The long, lavender eyes of Mother Nature glare at us,
And the rain continues to pour.

Rain and Death,
Like tea and sympathy,
Are a match made.

RAIN CORPSES

Many of these people in shades and shrouds of black
Look very familiar.
Perhaps it is just the cocktail party atmosphere
That creates this sensation of deja vu.
We view the raindrops and small talk
As minor annoyances—
Things not to have at our parties.
We all wish that we had been on the "uninvited" list.
And that we could have left our umbrellas at home
With the babysitter.

JESUS STREET

This morning I passed Jesus Christ
Standing on a street corner.
I walked unbelievingly past Marilyn Monroe
Not once, but fifty times.
(She was always in a different dress.)
Everyone is a savior or a starlet
In these whorey days of winter.
Prostitution wages war on insecurity—
A fight it's sure to win.
We hide among the individuals,
And pick sunflowers in the night.

COUNTRY THOUGHTS

Are you hiding behind haystacks
In the country?
Or, have you burrowed underground
With the potatoes and the turnips
To plan a revolution?
I take my combines to the field
To ravish and destroy—
To dig you up at any price.
Stinking, lousy crop this season!
Next year I'll plant mirrors.

M__Y

M__y,
The first star each night is for you.
I really don't know what to do
When you're not near me
To steer me through our skies,
And through your eyes.
The night crashed into day.

M__y,
The first dream each night is of you.
I hope you dream of me too.

M__y,
Tomorrow's first kiss....

(n.t. n.d.)

I'm beginning to realize
That LIFE is not like the movies
Although I often wish
I could sit in a darkened room
And watch myself traipse through my misadventures
Instead of doing the actual traipsing.

OVER YOU
(For M__y with apologies because I don't want to be over you.)

Basking in self-pity and the sun
I wonder which one
Will destroy my brain cells quicker.
I could always turn to liquor
But I'm morally opposed to drinking.
I'd like to find the answers
But I don't feel like contemplation.
Desperation is here to stay.

Oh, I'm…Oh, I'm over you.
After all the things you did behind me,
Even though your beauty still blinds me,
I'm. Oh…I'm over you
Drifting out of a drunken stupor
(Something about recovering from my morals).

DROWNING BROTHERS

I remember drowning at the age of two or three
And deciding to accept the water of the pool
As my burial robes.
I tried to fight, but the water confused me.
It was so blue in every direction,
And my concept of up and safety was lost.
Seconds seemed like hours.
The next thing I remember is looking at a photograph
Of me dripping and clinging to my brother.
Why my mother and a camera were at hand
When I was gasping for air and life
Is something I will never know.
I did not know gratitude yet,
So I simply clung and was photogenic.

At times now in a house without a pool,
My parents will throw me a line
And tell me to talk to my brother.
The conversation is like a ripple
In a shallow pool.
"How's the practice?"
"How are your cats?"
"How's the weather?"
Everything is fine and I'm so glad to hear it.
You can drown in an inch of water.

DROWNING BROTHERS (Revised)

I knew that my brother and my mother
Were in the yard nearby
When I, at the tender age of two,
Decided to tackle our pool alone.
I also knew, as I began to sink into the water,
That one of them would come and rescue me.
And sure enough, my brother jumped in
And pulled me out, and my mother spanked me;
But not until she had taken a picture of me
Dripping and clinging to my brother.
Why the camera was anywhere near the pool
Is something I will never know.
After the photo session, I went into the house to sulk,
And Mom and Mike went back to the yard.

When I look at the resulting picture,
I see that I knew no gratitude at the tender age of two.
My brother simply looked bored after his heroic feat.
He had had eleven more years than I
To learn how to be bored.
When I look at this picture,
I sometimes wonder if I should consider Mike a savior.
I'm sure that is not a role he wants.
Sometimes I wonder if he wanted the role of brother.
Eleven years and a lot of miles separate Mike and me.
I feel no sadness over this.
I wonder if he does. Maybe I should ask him.
That would give us something to talk about.
Maybe I should ask him why he saved me
At the tender age of two.
Was it because I was his brother
Or because I was a person?
Maybe I could find common attitudes towards life
That are stronger than blood
That is supposed to make us close.
That conversation could be the beginning
Of our relationship as men.

THE DINNER OF NEVER ENDING COURSES

As you walk out the door,
Don't think you're the final meal.
Even though I lie writhing on the floor,
I won't die from the digestion of your departure.
I will don my cellophane clothes
And prepare another course.
All the ingredients will be right—
Such a vain pantry—
But it won't be my decision
If this cake will rise or fall.

ODE TO SCIENCE

I know your face—
For its perfect angles have cut me,
And left me scarred.
I know your name,
But I don't know what's in it.
I know where your house is,
But I don't know where to find you.
Are you underneath the water,
Beneath the waves?
Or are you in the trees
Searching for the perfect leaf?
Oh, yes—I know your closet too.
I know your closet more intimately
Than either of us would like to admit.
However, faces and closets are not enough today.
King of Nature!
King of Dissection!
I know nothing of your cells and pores.
Today I must play scientist
And catch you in your habitat.
I must put you in a jar with chloroform
So I can study your every move and breath.

I need to label you, and put you in a drawer.
I need to know; I need to understand.

Only then can we begin.

I SING SONGS

Everyone I ever wanted
Is all tied up
In convenient wrapping paper
(under killer Christmas trees)
With manipulative bows
(For the killer birthday parties).

> Chorus:

I sing songs black, I sing songs white;
But my room is always quiet
Because no one sings to me.
I sing songs dead, I sing songs red;
But the color's always me.
The color that's left is always me.

Everyone I ever left
Is dragging behind me;
I can't erase their names
(They're silent balls and chains).
I can't discard their faces
(They're silent robes of steel).

> (Chorus)

Everyone I ever lost
Haunts me slyly in the night.
I can't sleep on my cross
(The silence reminds me of your words).
I can't sleep with the light on
(Because I'll only see everything that's gone).

IN YOUR TOWN I DON'T KNOW

I don't know how to drive in your town,
I don't know how to drive in your town anymore;
I don't know how to drive,
I don't know how to drive.
    All the roads are familiar;
    I just don't know the limits and the laws.
    I'm just waiting for the handcuffs.
    Why don't you chain me to the book
        Because I don't know how to drive?
    I don't know; I don't know.

I don't know how to speak in your town,
I don't know how to speak in your town anymore;
I don't know how to speak,
I don't know how to speak.
    I know what you say;
    I just don't know the replies.
    Why don't you revive me—resuscitate me—
    Mouth-to-mouth me words to say
        Because I don't know how to speak?
    I don't know; I don't know.

I don't know how to die in your town,
I don't know how to die in your town anymore;
I don't know how to die,
I don't know how to die.
    Hell!! Your dirt is so exclusive,
    Why don't you comfort me?
    Why won't you bury me
    In your high-rent graves
        Because I don't know how to die?
    I don't know; I don't know.

LOVE CHUNKS
(For __ with love)

At the strangest times
You hit me in the groin.
And I feel as if
I will throw up half a million days.

And this is not vomit from which I can walk away.
I have to stay and smell it burn,
And contemplate each chunk.

No antacid could calm my savage stomach.
And each time you pass
You smile and whisper,
"If swallowed, induce vomiting."

I AM
(For ___)

I think you forgot to tell me something
Before you ran out of my house,
And I think you might have been crying
As you sped away in your car.
That is fine for you.
You can make ice cubes with your tears
And put them in your next drink.
I am left with the dents your body made in my furniture,
And the opinions you gave of the music I played
When we made love.

MAN LIKE THE MOON
(For ___)

You remind me of the moon;
But neither one of you gets closer,
No matter how much I wish,
Even though you both are always there.

When you go behind a cloud,
I never know if you will be back.
When you go into your secret places,
I am left with a feeling of unknowing.

My prayer is the same
When either one of you is gone or hidden.
I pray for blindness; I pray for lack of hearing
So I will not have to know the world
Without your dual presence.

Scientists being mute
(That prayer's been answered)
I have no proof that you'll be back.
For all I know you could choose another orbit
And leave me drowning in freed salt water.

Dear homing pigeon, you always come back.
Not daylight, nor clouds, nor houses we could never call home
Can hide you from my view forever.

Maybe miles are the perfect distance.

PICTURE OF ___

My disc camera could never do you justice,
So I will take a picture with my mind.
While processing your picture,
I'll use all the colors of the summer I turned 19
One hundred times or more:
Green for youth, and lots of yellow—
Even though I detest the color.
It will take a lot of courage
To use every shade of blue I need;
But this is the only picture I will ever have,
So I'll have to make it perfect.

HAPPY TO BE STUPID

The feathers in this pillow
Come from birds I have not met.
And I do not know the sheep
Whose wool was used to make these blankets.
Likewise I do not know the woman
Who gave birth to the arms that hold me tightly.

Aware only of my lack of knowledge,
I willingly drown in the mattress
And let the blankets smother me.
I'm in Heaven as you cuddle me in your sleep.
(I hope you know it's me.)
I refuse to wake you and ask you silly questions.

PROMISES FOR THE PROMISED LAND

In a more beautiful place than this,
I would lick your sweat from the walls
And tremble my fingers to my lips
To bring it back to you.

In a more perfect place than this,
I would give you all my clothes
And put my masks away.
Though these masks may tell more
Than reality ever could.

In a more quiet place than this,
I would tell you all my secrets
And all the lies I've ever told,
And deliver my voice in a box to you.

Nothing more would need to be said
In a better place than this.
I could even give away my eyes and ears.
Just leave me with my thoughts and hands
And I think we would be very satisfied.

MORNING SICKNESS

Nausea walked in and took control,
And decided she didn't like the placement
Of my furniture or the arrangement
Of my closet. So everything was moved
Without me being asked.

As I sit in my displaced chair,
I wonder if I inquired
How you feel this morning.

AFTER AN EIGHT COURSE MEAL OF YOU

As you walk out the door,
Don't think you're my final meal.
Even though I lie writhing on the floor,
I won't die from the digestion of your departure.
I will don my cellophane clothes,
And prepare another course.
All the ingredients will be right
(Such a vain pantry),
But it won't be my decision
If this cake will rise or fall.

AFTER BEING MUGGED
(For my attackers)

I hope you are not huddled
In some dark corner of this city gloating
For it would be in vain.
Except for three small cuts
(Which soon will heal)
You have not touched me.
Except for a naked arm
(Which once wore a watch)
You have not stripped me.
Besides, the ticking of my heart and brain
Make up for the silence of my arm.

I must tell you that I still smile
At strangers on the street,
Even though they may be different shades of you,
And I have yet to buy a gun or a can of mace.
I've had no nightmares
And your faces on the inside of my eyelids
Have not kept me from beloved sleep.
I still walk alone at night.
No, that's not an invitation;
It's just a fact.
Someday I may again offer rides to strangers
And take them to darkened, unknown places—
A courtesy I showed last to you.

You have my watch
And a tiny portion of my pride.
(Let me tell you I have pride to spare.)
You choose to gloat?
I'll have you know I gloat too
For all I have retained.

STILL SUMMER
(1987)

There are now a million people
In the place where we were two,
And your face has become a blur
Of everyone who has passed me.

When I am at home
I lie on the floor,
And breathe with it—
The lie of happy houses.

When I'm in the town
(which I once found so large),
I pretend I'm in a carnivorous city
About to be swallowed and digested.

Gone from house and town, I still cannot find you
Even though I have the advantage of a distant view.
Maybe I'm the one who's hiding.
Did you know you're supposed to find me?

FOR ___—I THINK—WITH CONFUSION

I had regrets all the way home—
Things I should have done.
Just like the littlest pig:
Wee, wee, wee.

I've wanted to cry all the way home,
But the tears wouldn't come.
The icemaker always learns to work just as the party's over.
I think that's another cruel joke on me.

I tried to forget all the way home;
But you have sunk your teeth into my car,
And pulled me backward through all the yellow lights.
Everything seems so dark in reverse.

FOR ___

We rolled like metaphors
Somewhere in your house.
Don't ask me where?
The brain, the bowels, the bladder—
All the rooms look the same to me.

We were in a circle
Somewhere in your house
Against your square furniture.
No ending and no beginning;
For eternity infinite,
But definitely not meant to be.

We were parallel
Somewhere in your house:
Lines destined not to meet.
In passing, however,
You left so many memories.

Will they ever name a theorem after us,
Or are we too easy to solve?

INVITATION NOT TO KNOW YOU
(For ___)

Are you trying to seduce me,
Or do you stand so close within the touch of my eyes
Because there is nowhere else to stand?
Is your pornographic dance simply for me,
Or is it a coincidence that I'm the only one looking?
Do you—as I have hypothesized to friends—
Get kickbacks from the various state mental institutions
To which I will retire
If you succeed in pushing me past the precarious edge
Of my suburban, subhuman reality?

A step into your world
Would be a giant step for me,
And I would have to arm myself
With all the books of Knowledge.
(I'd need a thesaurus to express myself.
I'd need a dictionary to explain myself.)
In this day and age, "Hi" has too many meanings.
In this day and age, "I just wanted to introduce myself"
Means too much—even with access to all the words of Man.
I'd have to hope that you'd accept my loose translations.
Even with all my questions answered,
And the initial steps towards introduction made,
I'm not sure I'd really want to sleep
Underneath the subtle, violent shades of your skin.
I don't really know if I'd want to move
Within the dangerous folds of your clothes.

I'm so afraid you would lose your charm
If I could be inside your eyes and deconstruct your thoughts.

Perhaps I should be content
To leave you in your melancholy repose so close.
You could be a god or a reminder
Of things that are better left untouched.
However, if you take one step closer,
I will eat you alive, and pick your remains from my teeth
Without the slightest hint of regret.

        (n.t., 9/6/87)

I think I made my mind up once,
But it quickly goes unmade.
I think I made my mind up once,
But my thought refused to stay.
    Oh, they say the golden years are fading,
    But I just don't think that's true.
    Oh, they say the golden years are fading,
    But they better not fade till I'm through.

I think everything would be easier
If I had walked a mile in my own shoes.
I think everything would be easier
If I wasn't told whose mind I should use.
    Oh, Monday morning comes too soon
    And I can't stop people from yelling at me.
    Oh, Sunday evening comes too soon
    And I can't stop the people from leaving me.

        (n.t., n.d.)

I dance to the beat of a different drummer.
I reflect the golden light of summer.
The major majority frowns and tries to stop
The wicked dance, but my soul
In a psychedelic-electric-orange-and-
Lime-green-Stephen-Sprouse body
Bounces merrily through life.

I know that looks sometimes deceive
And all that glitters is not gold.
That's what people need to be told.
When the careless talk of how wicked I am
Becomes too much, and I am at my lowest ebb,
I laugh away the tears
And get back into step with my beat.

WINTER'S BACK
(3/3/88)

I am not into this ice shit.
I am not into this not being in control shit.
I do not like my legs being teased by spring
Only to go whimpering back
To the safety of long underwear.
Ice is everywhere and I hate it.
I was not made for these Death months.
I do not have enough fur for warmth
And I'm getting colder every day.

Ice is in my way and waiting
For me to fall in front of people
I would not care to meet this way.

I doubt my car will start.
I will have to walk till spring.

SHORT THOUGHTS OF ___

Your roots must be tired now.
They don't know what color to grow.
They're anxious for you to make up their minds
And reach for another bottle.

I'm sure you took those trips
Because no one was ever home.
(I know I wasn't.)
Empty houses weren't your style.

But now with passport and visa gone,
I think—hope, pray—you're learning to stay
With all those suitcases packed and empty.

I can see you crying
As the doctors asked for answers
That were not theirs to have.

I'm glad your house is clean without a doubt
And you won't have to vacuum
The dirt you feared so much.
I would have loved that dirt if it were mine.

I will always return to your hair
Though my fingers don't live there anymore.
I loved paying rent.
You were such a fair landlady.

DEALING WITH THE NIGHT

I need help too, ___ ___.
In that respect you are not alone.
However, nineteen years of extreme youth
Have made it hard for me
To know what my problems are.

I think we've shared some sleepless nights.
I've waited in bed for sleep to make his social call.
I've watched the ceiling remain absolutely still.
For poetry's sake, I've pretended that the stars
I see from my bedroom window are the eyes
Of people who have set goals for me.
These eyes glare and remind me
That I've done nothing with my day.
Insomnia is my punishment, I'm sure.

On the other hand, I also have a fear of sleep.
I'm afraid that if I accept the invitation,
I'll be whisked away by the limousine of night

And miss so much.
There's so much to miss
When you're just nineteen.

I need a voice, ___ ___.
I want to learn a language
That everyone can understand.
Maybe I should go to a big city
Like New York or London
And walk naked through the streets,
And absorb everything that passes me,
And will myself into becoming
A universal person.
Then, maybe I could help people everywhere
With their dealings with the night.

I want to be a savior.
I have known the sins of both sleep and insomnia.
I'm as close to an expert of these sins
As anyone would be.
I want to help people sleep without guilt
And lie awake for nights without fear.

I want to be a savior, ___ ___,
But I haven't got the right clothes.
I've wandered the streets of Columbia
Late at night,
And looked in all the shop windows.
No one is selling halos.
Ralph Lauren hasn't designed angel's wings
    Yet.

IN THE LANDSCAPE OF YOUR HOUSE

The stairs to your bedroom
Become a mountain.
I stop to see if there are wildflowers
Growing in the grassy carpet.
I drag the walls with my hands

To bring air with me
To this higher altitude.
I have never risen so high.
Your room is a plateau
And I can see for miles and miles
In all directions and perspectives;
I tell myself that I am the original pioneer,
Even though I know love like this has existed before.
It is a long walk through the history of romance
To your bed—a cloud.
I stagger through the wilderness
And fall in my destination—Heaven.
Your heavenly bed is a cloud
Of white sheets and feathers
And it's a happy place to be.
But I had no map to reach this place
And I'm not quite sure how
I'll return to the lands I know.

It's a jungle going back.
Wild grasses tear at me when you say good-bye.
Quicksand tries to eat me as you decide whether to let me go.
I avalanche down your stairs
And the ocean of your living room pitches me to the door
And onto the deserted island from whence I came.

TUCKERTON AFTER MEETING

My mother doesn't understand
When I say this picture frightens me.
There is something menacing
About this group of summer Quakers
(for that is the only time
they were near a place of worship)
Leaving their meeting house.
The New Jersey sun must have caught them unaware
After the darkness of prayer
Because they squint
And their mouths are too hard.

Ellen holds a doll
And Uncle Henry holds his hat.
His other hand is on Ellen's shoulder.
Does he think she'll run away?
Or is he pushing her closer to the Packard,
Sooner to the summer house
For another afternoon of swatting
Not yet legendary mosquitoes,
Nearer a bought debut,
Three children and a broken marriage?
The women in the picture
Should have followed Uncle Henry's lead
And taken off their hats.
Instead they are hidden beneath the brims.
They could be strangers.
They are saved only by the inscriptions
On the back of the photograph.
I can tell Kirk doesn't have his sense of humor yet.
And in this picture my father looks just like me.

UNSATISFIED TREES

The trees grow where the sky rests upon the earth.
They rise toward Heaven, knowing it is a better place.
And though blue and the clouds urge them upwards,
They cannot be tempted.
They are trapped with the dung and the soil
And Gravity's other adopted sons and daughters.

When the time comes,
Leaves will fall
To the waiting ground

Until that day, they cling like desperate children
To the serpent limbs, and twist with the branches.

They know they will never quite arrive.

LEARNING TO SWIM

Yucca plants and swimming pools
Crowd every suburban back yard
In Gainesville, Florida.
It's 1970, and I'm just two.
My father leads me to the edge
Of our pool. The water is blue,
Like his eyes,
And I'm afraid of falling,
So I just stand by,
And my brother screams,
"Just dive in!"
But I can't dive in,
So Daddy glides me in,
And my brother laughs
As I kick and gasp.

I swallow water and frustration.

I want to live to see three
And I want to be my father's fish child,
So I accept the motions of his arms,
And I breathe through him,
And I learn to swim.

NOT DELIRIOUSLY HAPPY, BUT PEACEFULLY CONTENT

Because it is summer and at 8:00 p.m.
The sun still plays here in Columbia, Missouri,
And I can wear sunglasses
Without becoming a fashion victim,
And speed excessively through the streets
And sing off-key to "Our Lips are Sealed,"
And drum my hands in perfect beat
On the steering wheel.

Not deliriously happy but peacefully content
Because it's hot but not humid
And I have the best of both worlds in my car—
With the AC on and the windows down.
I'm cool and free—a combination
Which makes me peacefully content,

But not deliriously happy.
Still, it was good to see the status
Of human perfection steer themselves
Across campus as I waited to register
For a summer class I might actually like.
They did all the humanly perfect things—
They always do—like be totally unattainable,
Which should make me deliriously happy
Because I wouldn't know what to do
With a statue in my bed
Although it would be fun to tell friends about.
But I can always lie
Which might make me peacefully content,

But not deliriously happy
Because my sweat was lonely this afternoon.
It wanted your fingers to tease
It to and from my private areas—
My brow and armpit among others.
Peacefully content because I know you're
Nowhere in this town, and that being with you
Wouldn't necessarily make me deliriously happy.

(n.t., n.d.)

I hate: work, school, living at home, being in debt,
being pawed, always having to make the first move,
AIDS, TV—except MTV and "Designing Women"
and news, funny things that aren't funny, being shy,
ugly clothes, muggy weather, taking classes because
I have to, queens!, people who call the Blue Note
"the note," not having fun talking to old friends,
people who can't keep secrets, people who nag

and/or whine, the Columbia Mall, hearing the same
music at Abs, pretentious people, bad music at bars,
music that is too loud at the bars, feeling fat,
ugly legs, not being in plays, feeling like I have to
get A's, being with people when I want to be alone,
sleeping with no AC in June, the smell of pot,
poppers, feeling like a nerd, red, frat boys who are
really, truly straight, analyzing something when I
want to keep my thoughts to myself, women's
sleazy underwear, waiting for people to call, being
reminded to do something an excessive number
of times, driving slow, parking tickets, talking
about sports or politics, people who ride bikes
in the traffic without thinking about safety,
drive-throughs, people who drag up things they
shouldn't know or who drag up things to
antagonize, being stared at when I don't want
to be, sweating.

I like: good humor, navy and white, being alone,
new tapes, new magazines, singing to myself
in funny voices, a full tank of gas, being in like
love, lust, etc., walking by A Cut Above in
my running tights, a good haircut, 5 Cape Cods,
a good band at the Blue Note, good music at
Questions, good audiences, flirting not in vain,
independent people with a sense of vulnerability,
hearing songs I love but haven't thought about in a while,
paychecks, no bills, no cavities, being recognized
for being in plays, my favorite books and stories,
crying at the end of Breakfast at Tiffany's and Out of Africa,
Lauren Bacall, Vivien Leigh, Judy Garland,
Ann Margaret, groovy 60's clothes, things I want
to be cheap or on sale, sleeping in the nude,
Prince cassingles, driving fast, zoinks, epuda,
Jessica in jeans and white oxfords, feeling
glamorous/chic, changing people's attitudes about
me, knowing what people really think of me,
staring, being younger than the people I am
attracted to, the 20's, sexy high-heeled shoes,

driving by myself, flying, beautiful eyes, talking
on the phone, shopping, white roses, Patsy Cline
and Guns N Roses, cleaning because I want to,
Belinda Carlisle on Carson or Letterman,
reading the paper in bed with breakfast, not taking
notes in classes I hate, doing important things for
myself not because I have to, taking walks around
UMC and downtown—alone, funny letters,
funny TV commercials, Zipps walk-up window,
being in on a secret or scheme, kissing, buying
stuff at Bennetons and Leos on the same day,
having the AC so cold in summer that you have to
snuggle at night, flirting as a joke, liking people
immediately, making people laugh and/or think,
people watching, being stoopid!, cheese, ketchup,
saying "thang of _____," Italian food, Iman, Cher,
Empire waists for women's clothes, antiques.

SEVEN REQUESTS

Take me to your slum.
Make me eat your garbage
And eight-course meal of lies.
Very fulfilling.
Oh, yes, I'm very satisfied.

Take me to your Heaven.
Put me in your dreams.
All Heavens—our heavens—are gifts
With strings attached intact.

Take me to your tenement.
Your hotel with many vacancies
Is such a very empty place;
But I can forgive you
For the room service is so excellent.

Leave me in your Hell on Earth—
Such a pretty picture.
Make all the bills conspicuous
So I can know the prices of your penis and balls.

(n.t. n.d)

Today I met a stranger in the bathroom mirror
Who said he didn't like me,
And said he would replace me with someone
Who knew what growing old was, and that
Time was something beyond the watch and clock.
The stranger told me to buy a book on loneliness
And read a book on pain,
And write a book about living
And then look at him again.

THE LAST NIGHT EVER IN MY GRANDMOTHER'S HOUSE
(Written on a piece of drawer lining paper)

No longer a home, barely a house;
Tomorrow is on the sidewalk
Wrapped up in boxes of old china and linens.
We wander through empty rooms,
That echo with silence, searching
For memories we stored for this moment.
In the corners, we find traces of yesterday
Swept up with the dust of today.
The room with a view shows forgotten faces;
Angular shadows whisper goodbye.

IV.

CHICAGO YEARS: ANOMIE AND HEARTBREAK

Rob repeatedly called his early weeks in Chicago a "blur," consumed by telephoning old friends, drinking bouts and picking up a series of male lovers. Occasionally he would chide himself in his journal for not pursuing theatre openings or trying to get a job. Recalling his college passion for acting opportunities, he asked, "What's wrong with me now?"

I was disappointed that he wasn't seeking a job and stunned that he showed virtually no interest in theatre, even as a spectator. We phoned each week for five years, arranged for him to make trips to join his cousin Ted in Texas, exchanged visits (particularly at Christmas), and generally tried to be supportive. Having heard of a psycho-social moratorium, I didn't despair; but I was desperately afraid he would ruin his health before he found his footing.

Resuming his journal some five years after arriving in Chicago, he wrote, "It is frightening to read old entries and see how little I've changed.... When will I ever learn to focus on myself and stop expending so much energy on trying to find a partner?" (He planned to break off with one infatuated lover that night, and then pursue a largely unresponsive, older man.)

In some respects, however, Rob had begun to succeed. Although he refused most of my offers to provide formal education or instruction, he took me up respecting acting lessons. Again and again these led nowhere, but he finally got part in "The Changeling," which played briefly in a very small theatre. We stayed in his rented rooms the night after the play—his first in five years. He was ecstatic.

After spending the $8,500 we gave him to get started, Rob hadn't been able to pay his rental-lease payments. (I told him I would not sign on for another lease.) He hadn't come home broke because he had become the lover of a well-to-do young man who provided for his needs. They eventually made a commitment to live together in a lover's relationship. Rob wrote us about his "gay" lifestyle, and was delighted to find that we were supportive—though not surprised. We visited them, and they visited us in Columbia. When his partner broke off the relationship, Rob was deeply hurt. They kept in touch, however, and Rob's later dreams and poetry expressed his continuing love.

Rob entered the work force as a telemarketer, unskilled data processor, and a waiter. For some years, he worked nights at a bar called "Berlin"—sometimes as the "bouncer." (This unlikely role, given his pacifism and gentle nature, must have been carried out with verbal persuasion although he had become quite strong from workouts in health clubs for six or more years.) Not only did Rob now pay his own rent, but he had acquired two cats from the break-up of his former committed relationship. These responsibilities troubled him when he got a chance to go to Los Angeles with an acting company. (Perhaps the exhilaration of appearing in "The Changeling" had inspired Rob to win a part in "Scenes From My Love Life"—a work of soft gay-porn. Despite my wife's dread of going to a large city and Rob's fear that we would object to his nudity on stage, we saw the play and praised his performance. Then the author-producer launched another play in the same vein called "Making Porn," and Rob played his part so well that he was asked to join a Los Angeles production for some 2 1/2 months.)

He declined, thinking that he couldn't afford to make the L.A. trip, but he hoped for another acting role soon. "I can't lose my momentum. I've been a working actor for several months straight and it has been great. This is what I want to do—despite my five years of doubts."

When he kept questioning his decision during August, 1995, several friends urged him to try L.A. The producers, he found, still preferred him to other candidates. I encouraged him to go for it and offered to pay his Chicago rent etc., while he was gone. His apartment manager promised to take care of his cats and his former apartment-mate in Columbia offered him a pad in L.A. So, he signed on for the gig.

During my years of guilt, I questioned encouraging him to enter the demoralizing L.A.-and tour-environments. But Chicago afforded him random, unprotected sex; group sex; and other perils. His co-workers at Berlin presented him with $250 in cash, and threw him a farewell party with shots and drugs that hurtled him "out of control." (He thought he might have become quite annoying, but couldn't remember enough to be sure.)

The L.A. performances, which attracted the movie industry's foremost porn stars, were popular. Rob was determined to make the most of the opportunity and put a positive spin on things—even the failure of his committed relationship:

> There are moments when I feel I am less over him than I thought I was. Maybe he let me go because he knew this was the life I was supposed to lead and that I could never be completely happy in Chicago with him. I do feel more on the right track than I have felt in a very long time.
>
> I can't believe I haven't had sex since I left Chicago. Amazing. This has been the longest time w/o it in years and years. I don't really have any overwhelming desire for sex. I want romance and friendship first. What a novel concept. Am so glad I'm out of the bar scene.... I basically feel really good about where I am right now.

Rob was still based in Chicago, but the success of "Making Porn" changed that. When the producers asked him to sign on for a West Coast tour followed by six or more months in New York City, he agreed.

Back in Chicago at the end of November, 1995, he wrote, "My last night in Chicago. Unbelievable. Numb. It has been non-stop since I got here." (He visited Berlin, touched base with a past lover, apologized to his former committed lover for not repaying certain loans and obligations, packed and loaded a trailer for me to drive back to Columbia.) He compiled a long list of Chicago associations, agonized over his failure to achieve a "stronger sense of who I am," and wrote "Leaving Chicago"—the poem that concludes this section.

Although Rob wrote relatively few poems while living in Chicago, he recorded several Chicago experiences and moods in future poems. (At times he was depressed over his rejections, his weight and acne, and his frustrated acting career.) Rob was patently alienated and insecure in Chicago—always feeling unworthy of its greatness. "The Foreigner" is his strongest Chicago statement of anomie whose echoes appear in other Chicago poems.

Unlike the tenderness in some of his college love poems, the references to love relationships in the Chicago poems are bitter—perhaps reflecting his rejections and the break-up of his committed relationship. Although he had some joys and successes in Chicago, Rob seemed paralyzed by anomie and heartbreak in the poems. As in Rob's high school writing, the poems portray a darker life than the journals—suggesting that his poetry was a means for venting frustrations.

WHATEVER YOU WANT—MAYBE

I am a softcore porn star
With tobacco-stained fingers.
I am your nightmare fantasy.
I can kiss you raw, but don't touch me.
And don't mess up my hair.
I'm hell on wheels without a car.
I don't wait for green lights;
I don't see red.
DON'T TRY TO LOVE ME;
Don't try to fence me in.

I'm a prima donna poster child
For your favorite charity.
I'll pose—I'll pout;
But not when you say please.
Walk on eggshells when you're near me.
Avoid my temper—avoid my stare.
I can be the train that never stops,
A plane that never lands;
But don't tell me that forever is what you want
Because I will leave you at the station
Alone with all your baggage.

THE FOREIGNER

My body lives in Chicago—
The land where buildings pretend
That they point to Heaven.
However, I think my heart and soul
Fell off the truck during the move
Through the wheat fields,
And I have to remind myself
That I am not a person watching a person
Watching all the people.
I am the original camera; I am here
Even though I am invisible on the EL.
If anyone finds a heart and soul

Lonely in a field with cows,
Please return them.
I'll gladly pay the postage.

          (n.t., 10/21/90)

I am the general of lost causes,
Dead horses, and burnt bridges.
I am the only soldier in this solitary battle.
I plot the campaign in my cozy tent
And do all the dirty work with my rusty bayonet.
It is an internal war—a civil war—
A battle between North and South.
An appropriate metaphor—if you think about it.
Think about it!

Neon scorches mark my trail
From Waterloo to Gettysburg.
What do I owe to Lee and Napoleon?
Corpses of captives litter the roads.
I always forget that the enemy is the enemy.

I try to turn him into something else:
A symbol of hearth and home.
But the enemy is fighting the same battles
On the same fields, so we forget our similarities
And we all end up under siege.
It's the costliest war in history,
And so many lives are lost,
And so many souls are lost,
And all the lives and souls are part of me.
Not enough of the little tin soldiers
Get to take that heartbreaking walk home.
Those that do are not impressed.

          (n.t., 10/21/90)

I waited.
That is one of my problems:
I wait at the wrong time

For the wrong reasons.
My friend Patience is so understanding
At the times when she should really walk out.
And when she should calmly wait
For the moon to fall out of the sky,
She huffs, and runs and loses the chance
Of owning the moon.

DEAD EARS

I have known (although not biblically)
Men who can't hear, men with dead ears,
So to speak, so to speak.
We use papers and pens.
When drunk, they slur their words in long hand
And they aren't much different from other drunks.
And when sober, they're eloquent writers,
And runners. And they run and leave me behind
In their proud dust. And I think
About their dead ears and my dead hands:
My hands that can't speak, my hands that just hang.

And I worry about losing my voice,
And I think about what's in their heads
Between those dead ears.
But I have sat in the hospitals of my mind
And seen acquaintances hover near death—
With dead hearts, and dead souls,
And dead brains. And I know
That dead ears aren't nearly as fatal.
So, all you young men with dead ears,
Run as fast as you can.
I'll try to keep up.

(n.t., 6/6/93)

I had a pretty thought;
But I let it slip away

And all the bad ones poured in—
More than the mind could hold.

Pretty thought, lovely thought,
Scamper back to me like a puppy.
Blow over me like a dust bowl—
Gritty dreams wash over me.
Cleanse away stark, austere reality.

Had a little dream
That on a isle I lived—
Water at my door—
Woke up in my kitchen
On my kitchen floor.

(n.t. 6/6/93)

I want to leave you now
And run across you
In the hazy future
In a seedy bar
In Rome or New York,
And fall in love with you again
In slow motion, when I can
Only be photographed in sepia.

DREAM

I would like to leave myself at home,
Go shopping, and buy clothes
Myself would never wear.

I NEED NEW APPLIANCES

When I have the courage to turn on my TV
I find the same show on every channel.
You know the show—the one where I walk in
And find him on my side of the bed.

Do you get cable?
What's the reception like on your TV?

When I take the plunge
And open up the refrigerator door,
All the food's the same.
Your know the dish—the one that's made
With all the ingredients you know I hate.

I know you order out.
I think I'll binge and purge.

(n.t., n.d.)

I was going crazy. I was stoned, lying
On my roommate's bed thinking how if
Only the Go-Go's were still a working
Band things would go much better.
I mean the Go-Go's are a fantastic band,
But could they really save the planet?
I knew I was going crazy. I knew
I was really stoned. I knew because
I was thinking if the Go-Go's
Could save the planet, I would want
To be the leader of the Go-Go's' revolution.
Think about it. Think about how great life
Was when the Go-Go's were really big for the first time—
'81, '82—before everybody started hating them for
No apparent reason—'84, '85. Maybe life was sucking
So bad in '84, '85—think about it—that the Go'Go's couldn't
Save us anymore. Maybe we didn't have enough faith.
Go-Go's reunite for real. Give us what you've got.
Save my sanity. Save the planet.

(n.t., n.d.)

I want to find the girl who I can
Hear saying, "Oh my God," on the bootleg tape
Of the Go-Go's' '90 concert at the Whiskey
When they start playing "Capture the Light."

I think she's got a New York accent.
At the Whiskey?
I want to find that wonder and surprise.
I want to find that happiness and remembrance.

I JUST WANT TO REASSURE YOU THAT YOU'RE MY FRIEND

Why?

Why what?

Why are you my friend or why
Do you feel like you're in 3rd grade?
Why do you feel you have to reassure me?

I just want you to know
In case you ever doubt the fact.
Okay?

Fine. Now get the fuck out of my face.

(n.t., 6/27/94)

You take away my sex.
I am not a woman.
I am not a man.
I am just one waiting to see you.

You take away my breath.
I am not living.
I am not dying.
I am just here, wondering if I want to be revived.

Since you have emotionally castrated me,
And taken away my air,
I wonder what will be your next steal.
I wait, oh so hopefully.

THE BERLIN* NAPKIN COMPOSITIONS

#1

The bar is silent; the bar is still.
Time freezes and lets its luminance
Bathe them in lightness.
Their laughter tumbles
Their touches slow and tough
Just like it should be.

      Chorus:

They got it right;
They got it good.
They're young lovers
Just like it should be.

He's so smooth;
He's so dark.
He runs, laughs
And runs right back.
He just drips now
Just like it should be.

      (Chorus)

He's so open;
He's so ready.
He brushes his hair
Out of his eyes
To get a better view
Just like it should be.

#2

Baby, you got a beautiful ass.
Shake it over, my baby.
Baby, shake that ass s'more
And tell me that you'll stay.

#3

Is there something I can get you?
Is there something that you need?
A cup of coffee? A rootbeer float?
Right away—it's coming up.
Oh, I can spare a quarter.
Oh, I can spare a dime.
Need a smoke? Here you go.
I'll strike the match, I'll catch the ash.
Hell, I'll even smoke it for you.

#4

Where were you when tomorrow
Seemed so bleak? Where were you
When the end was near
And I chose not to repent?

I think I'll pack it up.
I think it's time to go
Open my umbrella
And float away.

* Berlin refers to the Chicago bar that employed the author.

LEAVING CHICAGO FOR L.A. IN A TEXAS ACCENT

I.

The ghosts brushed by me
As I shoved outta town.
Your ghost is everywhere
    Here.
Your ghost will be everywhere
    There.
   But There
He will wear swimming trunks

And be
Very, very muscular.

II.

I got high,
And I flew,
And I dreamed like a baby
That I had a life here.

III.

In Chicago,
The kids swing rope.
In LA,
I'll sling hope
In an Italian restaurant.
So far.

IV.

Lots of little
Epiphanies
    Lately.

V.

And it would've probably made me cry
    If I had let it.
So I didn't let it.
And I sang that Mary's Danish song
As I stomped out of this town.
(I'll never leave Chicago.)

VI.

I edited the things
That woulda made me
Sound too stoned.
(I edited the things I forgot.)

VII.

Looked in the mirror that you gave me.
Found out who I was.
And I left cuz I was ready.

VIII.

Ready to leave Chicago.
LSD's* gonna kill me.
It'll probably make me cry,
But I'll let it.

IX.

A quick good-bye kiss
To who I was.
And I was ready to leave—
Almost.

X.

I said goodbye,
So I didn't call
To say goodbye
    Again.
But I wanted to.

XI.

Do you live in Chicago?
Not anymore.
Where'd ya move?
Los Angeles.
This'll be an easy cab ride, right?
Yes, at this time.

XII.

This is for you
Because you
Are here.

XIII.

I was a B-movie queen
In the back of the cab
As I wept
At your movie-star glamour.
I never could compete
With you.

XIV.

I'm leaving Chicago.

*LSD refers to Lake Shore Drive whose beauty "always killed me."

V.

ON TOUR: ACTING KUDOS; MORAL RUIN

After rehearsing in L.A. during December 1995, which briefly triggered Rob's fear of failure, "Making Porn" played in L.A., Palm Springs, San Diego, Sacramento, and San Francisco before moving to New York City the following May. Rob wanted to make a permanent home for himself and his "girls" (two beloved cats), who were being housed by L.A. friends; but the tour took priority.

Jerry (Hello Dolly) Herman liked the show when it played Palm Springs. Rob's face was now clear of acne; but he sank awfully low there, in sharp contrast to his positive lifestyle during his brief L.A. adventure the preceding fall. Besides heavy drug and alcohol abuse, and pursuing such male lovers as the "sensual mechanic" and the "hot leather man" (cooled by a golden shower), he began the "hooking" referred to occasionally in his poetry. Here's how he described part of an "especially pleasant" 36 hours:

> Monday night, I turned my first trick. I can't believe how good I feel about this. This guy was cruising me at Tool Shed. Bought me a beer. Asked me out for dinner. After dinner, back to his place and he started pawing me. I said I enjoyed dinner but that I was a working boy. $100 an hour. I got $200 and

only "worked" an hour. Just jacking off. Hell of a lot better than waiting tables. Definitely an avenue to pursue. And I feel no guilt or shame.

After discussing the hooking (escort) trade with a cast member, Rob decided that he wouldn't mind the act (ever the "kinkier stuff" that the "pretty boys" wouldn't handle); but dreaded failure—"another aspect of rejection." Perhaps few gays would pay for his "services," but "I have a big dick. That's really what it's all about." Since he wanted more money so that he could have a life while acting for low pay, he'd risk rejection. "I don't want to work some shit job for even one minute more."

Throughout his year of touring, I urged Rob to find part-time work to meet expenses, move toward financial independence, and hopefully to keep him out of self-destructive pursuits. Back in L.A. between trips, Rob picked up his back pay from waiting tables. "$200 for two weeks of grueling work." he wrote. "Puts the escort thing in perspective since that is what I made for about two hours of work." Hooking wasn't always so lucrative however. (In San Francisco, he got $20 for letting someone suck his dick, and $50 when another client "gave me head." Not the preferred rates, but "beggars can't be choosers.") He also wanted to sell nude photos to a magazine—hoping for $400. When Rob needed money for necessities, however, he got it from me or one of the producers.

There were times of acute distress. As Rob was sobbing in Balboa Park, his best chum in the cast told him that this was a time for him to be alone. ("I don't want anyone to touch me or get inside me. My focus needs to be on me.... It will be a while before I can even fathom dating.")

And there was a slapstick moment on stage in Sacramento, which "broke us all up." Rob, playing a sadistic "leather man," pretended to suck sperm then regurgitated milk. At this point, a cat ran up on stage, "so, as I walked off dripping with milk, I yelled, 'Here kitty, kitty, kitty.' Hysterical."

Coming off several weeks of sell-outs in San Francisco, Rob was very eager to continue with the show to New York City. During the layover in LA., he met his dream man who would haunt him for the remainder of his days. Taking off for New York in mid-May completely stoned, he lamented that one of his cats named Kate, whom he had left with a male friend, had become incontinent. Still stoned the following day, he wrote his first New York poem about a McDonalds.

For nearly a month, "Making Porn" was in the preview stage—with large audiences—before its official opening on June 12. When the theatre air conditioning failed, the producers substituted fans blowing over buckets of ice. After a producer promised him $20 per month for the purpose, Rob finally got a haircut. At the end of May, while my wife was on a walking tour in England, I took him to the Picasso portaiture exhibit and enjoyed the play with the air conditioning working and the bath rooms not flooded. Rob was so good I was humbled. As I spoke with the author and his co-producer afterward, I was so elated that their praise added nothing.

But Rob had mixed feelings:

> I guess our entire visit went o.k.; he just stresses the fuck out of me. He gave me some money, but I was hoping for a lot more. I am so horrible! He had a whole list of possible jobs I could take to earn some extra money. None of them had much appeal.... I don't know if we listen to each other very well. Sometimes I think he doesn't understand me at all. I'm probably just really fuckin' spoiled.

He was quite right that I didn't understand him; his journal later shocked me.

Rob did such drugs as marijuana, crystal (mathamphteamines), and crack cocaine. Influenced by a high school friend, he broke his rule against getting stoned before play performances. He practiced hooking in reverse, repeatedly paying $10 to get sucked. On the plus side, he refused a request from an HIV+ lover to be fucked without a condom. Having a life meant plenty of money for such vice plus bar-hopping. When we gave him $100 for his July 9 birthday and the co-producer did the same, he spent the money fast. Frustrated by failure to catch on with an escort service, he wrote, "I'll have to check out other agencies or—gasp—think about getting a real job. Got paid yesterday, and it is already almost gone. Not a surprise."

Much of this journal dissects the workings of his theatre company; but he was perhaps most concerned with keeping in touch with both his former committed partner and his California lover. (He kept wondering how the California relationship, based on four dates, would survive the separation.)

Rob did roller blade in Central Park and take occasional trips around the city. A woman from his Berlin days took him out to lunch with no dissipation involved. Although he spoke of loathing his body, he also said he liked what he saw in the mirror—referring to his overall life. His acting was praised by the media and some theatre buffs. He was asked to appear in a low-budget movie, in which he played a porn star interacting with a female who hadn't been informed that her role required semi-nudity. The costumer told Rob that male porn underwear would be desirable for the second day's shooting. The director, however, was scandalized when Rob wore a leather jock strap. (I don't know what happened to this film.)

After Labor Day, Rob's life became a melodrama. He yearned for a homosexual "marriage" and a home with his cats, where he could accumulate art works and antiques. Sensing that he would probably not long remain a cast member in "Making Porn," he groped for ways to achieve his goals. Like a soap opera, this quest involved simultaneous sub-plots.

After roughly 10 months of working together, tensions within the cast increased and the producers became critical of their performances. A lead actor told a mag that his co-actors were dragging down the show. The author-producer, who also acted and directed, cut back his participation then reasserted himself forcefully. Certain actors—including Rob from time to time—got high before performances; one show was nearly canceled because a stoned actor was so late in arriving. But training understudies caused uneasiness.

Rob's emotions jangled from ongoing communications from his former committed partner, who had moved to Maine along with Rob's second-most adored lover from his Chicago period. Rob knew his former relationship was over, but the wound was kept smarting.

Rob kept his California relationship going, but his protestations of love were not reciprocated. Hope for a "marriage" probably was the key factor in Rob's decision to return to L.A. whenever he left the show. The Californian finally made a trip to New York to visit a man he loved, and Rob socialized together with them. When the Californian was hospitalized, Rob was most attentive during his convalescence; the third party was not. With no commitment to Rob, the Californian renounced the other man before returning to L.A.

Having patched together his relationship with the other man, the Californian returned to New York to see him. And he also wanted to see Rob, who was having crises of his own. First, his two best chums in the cast were fired. Then Rob—the last member of the original cast except for the author-producer—received his dismissal notice and lacked money for a fresh start.

When the Californian invited him to lunch, Rob could not accept because he had a hooking engagement. (He was receiving $300 per call and had a repeat client.) After placing an ad for his services, he learned by phone that the police were answering such ads. Rob was alarmed—perhaps without reason since his informant was a rival hooker. He received flowers at his last of 370 performances of "Making Porn," and the author-producer praised him during the curtain calls. With a $500 severance bonus, he left New York with about $1,100. (He was still negotiating with two women in L.A. for a pad. One was his former room mate and previous benefactress who had become so disgusted with caring for his incontinent cat, plus his other cat, that he had given permission to have them destroyed. Would she?)

In both the journal and the poems written during his touring period, Rob wrote simply and realistically, with few traces of the lurid surrealism of his high school days. Occasionally, he was humorous or expressed his sensitivity. While wrestling with the issue of leaving New York, he said:

> Been thinking about how beautiful Chicago was when winter turned to spring—the first blades of new grass, brilliant blue skies after months of grey. I bet New York is a lot like that. Wondering if I'm making the right decision.

Again and again, he expressed his fears of failure and the unknown.

Most of the poems in this section, beginning with "Five Long Years," are either self-lacerations or descriptions of unrequited love from specific persons. Only a few are humorous or tender. Three of the concluding poems deal with impending changes for the better in his life—a great concern for months before his November departure from New York. A short poem (10/25/96) looks beyond hooking to the "next transformation." In an obvious repudiation of hooking, "Things are Gonna Change" expressed a desire for moral maturity and a determination to put personal relationships on an unselfish basis.

"Rogues and Vagabonds," however, packed his yearning for "marriage," a home and financial independence into the word "stability." The title had "been tumbling around in my head for months." He spent an uncustomary length of time on revisions because "I'm trying to record this past year and a half in a poem, and it is somewhat elusive." Again he had come to a turning point, reassessed his life and prepared to move on. This time he pointed himself toward "square one."

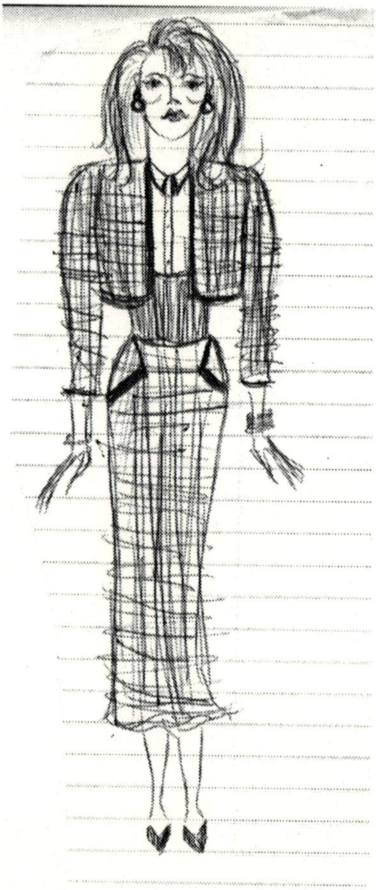

Robert Charles Jones, with biographical material by Bartlett C. Jones

FIVE LONG YEARS

For five long years
I didn't move,
I didn't talk; I didn't breathe.
For five long years
I didn't feel.
I let my heart become a sieve.

For five long years
I forgot the stars.
For five long years
I worked in bars.
For five long years
I forgot the sun; I forgot the sea.
Forgot, forgot and silenced
All the things that were really me.

For five long years
I was a blank—
An open sore
That smelled so rank.
For five long years
I became a ghost,
And in my haunting,
Disrespected my host.

(n.t. n.d)

Blonde accountant, green thumbed:
Beyond blue, blue eyes
Imperfect truth, but flawless skin.
We met in a dark, adult bookstore
And decided to take our shenanigans
To the respectability of my place or yours.
Mine—it turned out: a place
To which you haven't ventured back.
In your bed, though, several times
We curled, curved back to front.
And you said it felt so good,

And I've never felt so safe.
But I didn't tell you this.
Maybe I should have.
You thought I had California attitude
(Whatever the Hell that is)
The first time you saw me.
You said I looked like
I had just come from dinner or a play.

Actually, I had been to a play; I starred in it.
It's called, "A stranger from Chicago goes to
A couple of gay bars and pretends to have fun
While surrounded by a lot of pretentious,
Gorgeous people who wouldn't give him
The time of day but would fuck him maybe
If they were really drunk."

It's a great play; you should see it.
Maybe you have.
How many real dates?
Two—a movie and New Years Eve.
May I count New Years Eve?
Please let me—plus a couple of
Extraneous nights thrown in there
For good measure.

Then the canceled date
And I haven't heard from you since.
And I don't know what to think.
I've never learned what to think about things like this.
Everything seemed so positive—
Why haven't you returned my calls?

THE NEXT (n.d.)

You are the next dream catcher.
You are the next reflector.
You are the next, but don't forget
He's more than your protector.

He's a boy so golden.
Do you watch him while he eats?
I always loved the way he kept one hand
Tightly in his lap,
While the other hovered 'bove the plate.

You are the next forever.
And, believe it or not,
I hope it's true.
He deserves boundless tomorrows,
Even if they're with you.

You, the next, don't forget
To hold on to his smiles.
Don't take for granted his embrace.
His soul is blinding, bountiful;
But it will fly for its own protection.

What can you do?
What can you do?
What can be done
To turn off the light
Of the wretched sun?

Don't want to see.
Don't want to feel.
Give me a minute,
Hear my appeal.
You can have both my eyes.
You can have both my hands.
If you take my soul too,
I'll do whate'er you command.

BREAKING THE SURFACE (n.d.)

You decided
It was time to breathe—
Time to let

This under-water tea party end.
You watched
The words "I love you"
Bubble from my mouth
One final time.
You exhaled, buoyed up,
And broke the surface.
You were
Golden in the sun.
Everything moves much faster
Above the water.
You were on the shore and dry
Before I realized
How much deprivation of oxygen
I could survive.

HUSH, HUSH

Stoned, or stone-cold sober,
Everything out of my mouth is silly.
I watch you fade out as I talk on.
I stop, beat back the words,
And pray you'll forget
I ever started talking.

WHO STOLE ME?

Who stole me?
Was it while I gently slept
That a black-clad burglar crept
Into my unsuspecting room
And spirited me away?
Did he pawn me?
Sell me for crack?
Hope he got a good price.
Was a ransom note ever left?
Did you even realize a theft
Had been committed?
The detectives are perplexed—

No signs of entry forced;
Not a finger print in sight.
Maybe it was an inside job.

BURIAL GROUND

I've buried many summer days
In the graveyard of my heart.
Stillborn Christmases
And Thanksgivings
When I puked the night before—
So drunk—
Lie buried side by side.
Centuries from now
The sands of time—
Those cliched, Goddamn sands of time—
Will hide all traces
Of this ancient burial ground.
Oh, let no archeologists
Disturb these tombs.
The mummies aren't for museums.
The hard-earned treasures
Buried with them
Aren't for some snob collector's den.

IN A FIRE

Isn't it cute
When people ask
The one thing
You would save
Were your house
To catch on fire?
The next time
Some idiot
Asks me that
This is what
I plan to say:
I'd gather up

All the things
That matter not
And toss them
In the yard,
And then go sit
Among the flames
With love letters
From an Irish lad
And the pictures
From our parties
And wait to become
A fucking, martyred phoenix.

FAYE MORRISON—1996

It's been a long time
Since I've seen your rolling curves.
Do you still love the smell
Of freshly mowed wild onions
In the twilight in August?

In December.
In the morning,
Does someone stoke your fires?
Do you shuffle through your house
Pausing momentarily
At frosted window panes
To watch the children sled?

It's been a long time.
Do you remember me,
Faye Morrison?
I'm one of the boys
Who slipped away.
If it's any consolation
As you're passing through your years,
We are the boys
Who love you most
Because we have that distance.

ON A CALIFORNIA NIGHT

I wish I could show you
The colors of the sky I'm seeing.

But I shouldn't be too disappointed
Because I know
Your eyes are always in me.

SHOW BUSINESS

Today is the second time
Since I've been in L.A.
That the Great Director
Has decided to unplug the sun,
And called for the technicians
To turn on the rain
And drop the scrim of grey.
I guess that's my cue
To act melancholy.

THIRTEEN MONTHS

It's been thirteen months
Since you held me as a lover.
You did the breaking;
But I was the one who left.
I've had three homes
In thirteen months—
None of them were mine.
How many beds in thirteen months?
All I know is—
None of them were mine.

I've looked in a lot of mirrors
In these thirteen months
Though none of them were mine.
I'm learning to like what I see.

Don't own anything except myself.
That's enough for thirteen months.

BLIND OR STUPID
(For ___)

The conviction of your decision
Took my breath away.
I was too busy gasping for air
To see you place the wings upon my back.

The determination in your voice
Filled my eyes with tears.
I was too busy sobbing despair
To see you tuck the map into my pocket.

The finality of your words
Robbed me of my senses.
I was too busy screaming,"No fair"
To see you hang the compass near my heart.

I HAVE A HISTORY

I woke up and discovered
That I have a history.
I am not just water covered by skin.
I am days and hours.
I am young women singing.
I am atoms, and Adams,
And neurons, and rivers.
I am success and desolation.
I am strong men and brave women
Who have blazed many trails.
I am dirt. I am the heavens.
I am all the skies I've crouched under.
I am a lover, a scholar, a shaman.
I am receptive.
I am my mother's books.
I am my father's lessons.

I am short stories, tall tales,
Non-fiction and lies.
I am many stages.
I am seconds.
I am glances.
I am second glances.
I am fine cheap wine.
I am broken glass.
I am the oracle
Of my twenty-seven years.
I am a keeper.
I am the highways of this country.
I am the pathways to my heart.
I am Marietta,
Gainesville, Fayette, Columbia,
Chicago and L.A.
I am dark bars.
I am green hills.
I am a mirror.
I am many, many file cabinets.
I have walked.
I have prayed.
I have dreamed.
And I have done.
You may never read of me
In school,
But I have a history

SENTIMENT

People have climbed this mountain
And left their mark on the terrain.
And this mountain has suffered
Mightily from the elements,
But it is still there.
This is not real deep poetry—
In fact, it's more like
Common knowledge,
But still...
So profound.

THE HOLLYWOOD SIGN

From where I stand
Hoping to make a buck—
Actually hoping to make
A hundred and fifty bucks—
I can see
Above the buildings
Beyond the trees:
The Hollywood sign.

I didn't set out today
To become a cliche.
Yet here I am:
Another starving actor
Leaning against a wall,
Trying to hustle his dick
Until he becomes a big star,
Staring at the Hollywood sign.

FOR ___

He was the boy
For whom there were
No in-betweens.
He was off;
He was on.
No in-betweens.
And when he goes,
No purgatory for him.
He's going straight to heaven.
Or straight to hell
Where, regardless of the destination,
He will be warmly greeted
And cherished by the current residents.

GHOST OF A PREPPY LOVE GOD STUD SCARED BY SATAN

Saw a boy today

On a bike today.
Looked a lot like you,
Enough like you;
But it wasn't you.
Same head up.
Same determination forward.

Saw a boy today
On the street today.
Looked a lot like you,
Enough like you;
But it wasn't you.
Same cocky walk.
Same khaki shorts.

Saw a boy today
In an old Ford truck today.
Not a thing like you.
Not a hint of you.
Not a scent of you.
He was Satan leaning in to
Hear the music.

SAME THING

Saw a boy I knew
Or one who looked like
A boy I knew
Which is entirely possible
In this neighborhood.

They all stand and wave
To boys who look like them—

Boys I'm not quite quick enough
To turn and see.

Waving to reflections of perfection,
They walk by me,
Ignore me, see through me.
We must not be acquainted;
But I know I know them,
Or boys just like them.

Same thing.

Wait long enough,
Stare long enough,
Forget enough, Give up enough,
And soon you know you'll find
The boy you really know.

Or the same thing as.

YOU THINK YOU'VE GOT A PROBLEM, ALANNIS?

Cruising Starbucks,
Cruising boys,
Sitting at Starbucks,
Cruising boys.
Finally got a smile…
From a lesbian.

NOTE TO STARBUCKS

Hey, Starbucks!
Among the mugs,
Among the teas,
Among the merrily wrapped
    Bags of coffees,
Why don't you sell some pens?
Some green Starbucks pens

With gold lettering
For tripping poets like me
Who want to write poetry.

And if you don't sell those pens,
Those green Starbucks pens
With gold lettering
Along with the other corporate shit you sell,
Tell your fucking employees
To not look at me
Like I'm from Mars
When I ask to borrow one.

A pen,
For like three minutes,
So I can write some
Tripping poetry
And maybe sell it
And make some money
So I can get out of
The Hellhole of my life
And buy some more
Of your overpriced drinks
And cruise boys in your cafe.
Boys who will never want me.
(Thank God, really
But I'm on a bitching roll.)
I mean I know
Pens go really fast
In the service industry.
A lot of things
Go really fast
In the service industry.

I just wanted it for three minutes
    (I'm not from Mars)
To write poetry.

I'm coming in for another glass
Of iced tea.

I bought a pen
Down the street.

You got me.

NAMES INGRAINED

"Chicago."
He said your name, "Chicago."
He said your name again.
I see you as locations in movies—
Movies I watch in beds,
In motels, on tour,
On permanent tour.
Full-time vacation.

___,
I hear your name all the time.
A scary introduction:
"Hi, my name is ___."
I still flinch when someone else
Speaks of a ___ they know.
Could it be my ___?
The same ___?
Not yet!
But your spirit is everywhere.

JOURNAL ENTRY, POETRY OR BIRTHDAY CARD?

Where's ___?
Waiting for ___.

It's his birthday.
Sharing parts of the day,
His day, with him.
Waiting for ___.
Can't be a burden.
Need a smoke.

I bet he's getting more
Than his hair cut off.
Cool for him!
I really mean it.
He got me high.
He got me stoned.
So I can wait for him.
Patiently for him.
The scenery's good.
Smoking's bad.
So I'll wait.
Smokeless.
Waiting for ___.

SOMETHING

You are beautiful
In your range rover.
You are beautiful
Behind that coffee bar.

Working it,
Or working class,
Or really, really rich—
I don't care.
Of course the ideal would be
A construction worker in a Biemer.

THE PESSIMIST

I won't see him again tonight.
Heading out he is
To see another boy
He doesn't want.
They'll probably do some fighting,
Or maybe they'll just fuck.
In any case.
I won't see him again tonight.

POEM TO McDONALD'S

It was the kind of McDonald's
Where people looked like
They wanted to join the old man
Singing with the muzak.
It was the kind of McDonald's
Where people traded newspapers.
It was the kind of McDonald's
Where the staff was intelligent and friendly.
Really!
It was the kind of McDonald's
Where people were not afraid to be brave.

(6/4/96) n.t.

I do the dance
That makes my muscles feel good
Like someone I like told me.
That somebody said,
"If I knew what the dance meant
I wouldn't need to do it."
That's a direct quote, I think.

WHO'S GOT LOW SELF-ESTEEM?

What do you feel
When you touch my skin?
What do you see
When you look at me?
Do your fingers trace the stretch marks?
Or is it cellulite?
Do you know I once was fat?
Do you know I hate my body?
Do you see the pits?
Do you see the scars?
Do you see the ingrown hairs?
Can you imagine looking in the mirror
And, instead of your reflection,

Seeing what I have to see?
Do you know that I loathe my face?
Do you see the crunches I do every day?
Do you feel the 45 minutes on the treadmill?
Do you know why I prefer aerobic
To anarobic activity?
Because no matter how thin I am,
I feel fat.
I see lard.
I see scars.
I am scars.

(8/6/96) n.t.

Let me tell ya'll a story
About a man I loved named ____.
We met and had four dates.
And then I moved
All the way across the country.
(New York, with a play. Don't ask?)
I wrote; he called several times.
And then once I called, and he said,
"Hey, there's a letter on the way,
With pictures like I promised."
He said, "Call when you get 'em."
I got 'em.
I called.
"I got the pictures and your letter."
He had company—
A guest.
How sad.
The end.

I'VE ALREADY DONE IT

I can beat myself up
Better than anyone can.
It'll all be over
Before you have a chance to strike.

I'll be bloody on the floor
Before you can cock your arm;
I'll be crying in the corner
Before you can raise your voice.
Don't waste your time trying to hurt me.
I love the dirty work.
I'm a martyr; I'm a selfish bitch.
I won't give you the pleasure
Of seeing my walls fall down—
Of seeing my jelly ooze on the floor—
Of seeing my light short out.
I've slept with the problems that are me,
So don't waste your breath
Trying to teach me how to live.
I know I'm a whore.
I've seen the reflection.
I know the ideal.
So silly, upstart child—
Put your rulers and mirrors away;
Save your time.
This corpse has already been dissected
With scalpels and laser beams
By the coldest, most clinical, most analytical
Hands of all—
My hands.

ROCK-N-ROLL HEARTBREAK

Well, you had a change of heart
So I had to change my mind.
I thought that things were cool,
But to you they weren't that fine.
I know that I've been bad,
But you haven't been that good.
Would you let me stick around
If I threw some wood?

I've been counting all the cards
So I know what hands been dealt.

I know I used to be in love
Cause in my heart you've dwelt.
But it's useless to ignore it
Cause all the facts are plain.
It's time for me to take that walk
Though a part of me remains.

Well, tomorrow is another day
And tonight's another night.
Put a six pack in his hand
And anyone is Mr. Right.
They say there're other fishes
Swimming in that sea.
Guess I'll just have to cast my rod
And find the one for me.

ROGUES AND VAGABONDS

We're fraying at the edges—
Who knows when we'll explode?
I wonder who'll not care tonight.
We're all alone and leaving
With no one to devour but each other.
But I remember when times were new
And words had magic
And we didn't hate the sound
Of each others voices.
And we didn't want to leave.

It's time for home and time for bed
And time to feed the kiddies.

I can't be on the road tonight,
Even on off-Broadway.
I haven't seen the stars in months,
And I haven't seen my cats.
But I'll always treasure our vagabond days,
Our days in the wind, our days without homes,

Our days with no roots—
The days full of sun in new cities.

No, I don't want another bump.*
I don't want another line.
I'll never stand in line for rejection again—
At least, not again today.
Next time I'll know when to leave;
He'll never make me cry again.
But I remember when our roguish ways
Brought smiles and giggles, and there
Was still innocence in our deviance—
At least, there was innocence in mine.

Whose turn is it to discover
We have only each other to devour?
I can sense our bodies changing.
We're harnessing our energies;
We're tapping our reserves.

Now it's time to find our homes
And it's time to make our beds.

I can see the compass turning,
Pointing to stability,
Pointing to square one.
My eyes are blinded by the metamorphoses.
We're picking up the pieces of the boys we used to be
And tying them to the shards of the men we have become.

*Bumped refers to replacement in the play by his understudy.

(10/25/96) n.t.

Well, I've been doing some hooking
So I could afford to buy some new tapes.
And I've even got some money stashed away
For the next transformation.

THINGS ARE GONNA CHANGE

On November third
I'm gonna cut my hair
And dye it blonde;
Lighten up my eyebrows,
Buy green contacts for my eyes;
Shave my goatee;
Get a tan—real or fake—
Just want new skin.
On November eighth
I'm gonna shed my hooker strut.
Gonna fly away and learn to walk
Like a man in the West.
Gonna teach myself again
How to touch another soul
Without expecting payment
(Though whether or not it's cash,

I think I've always expected payment
for my touch.)
Maybe I'll quit smoking.
Nah!
Maybe I'll be a drunk again.
Haven't been a drunk
In a long time.
The recent storms have been created
By another type of tropical depression.
By the middle of November
I'll be resting in Missouri—
Restoring in Missouri.
No worry; no hurry for a while.
Then things will change again.

MY NAKED BODY

Thousands of strange men
Have seen my naked body.*
And most of them have paid.

I've been a whore for art
And a whore to save my life.
Either way someone else
Has reaped the profit
From my naked body.

*He played nude scenes in his last two plays that toured the nation.

ROGUES AND VAGABONDS
(revised)

We're fraying at the edges.
Who knows when we'll explode?
I wonder who'll not care tonight—
Who will transform tonight.
Whose turn is it to discover
We have only each other to devour?
I can sense our bodies changing.
We're harnessing our energies.
We're tapping our reserves.
> But I remember when times were new,
> And words had magic,
> And we didn't hate the sound
> Of each other's voices,
> And we didn't want to leave.

Now it's time to find our homes,
And it's time to make our beds.
I can't be on the road tonight—
Even on off-Broadway.
Even on off-Broadway,
I haven't seen the stars in months.
I can see the compass turning,
Pointing to stability,
Pointing to square one.
> But I'll always treasure our vagabond days—
> Our days on the wind—
> Our days without homes—
> Our days with no roots—
> The days full of sun in new cities.

Oh, what a lifetime we have lived
In this one short year.
I hope you hang on to the memories
Of the things I have edited or forgot.
Some day I want to compare notes
On our lives led far from the straight and narrow,
But now my eyes are blinded by the metamorphoses
In front of me.
We're picking up the tender pieces
Of the boys we used to be.
Tying them to the shards of the men we have become.
> But I remember when our roguish ways
> Brought smiles and giggles,
> And there was still innocence
> In our deviance—
> At least there was innocence in mine.

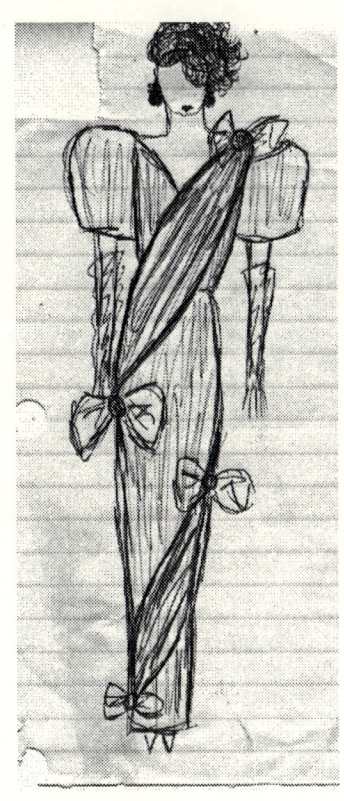

VI.

L.A.: LOVELORN LAMENTS IN SURREAL SETTINGS

The month that Rob spent with us, with time off for a trip to see his cousin in Texas, was a prelude to his L.A. residency. His future there, and his hopes for a "marriage" with the Californian he so admired, had troubled him deeply during his final weeks in New York. But three of his New York poems show he was hoping for a personal transformation. ("Feel like I'm shedding a skin. Have been feeling rather beautiful lately.") Leaving the city by bus, he stopped writing in his journal to "watch New York City fade away." He recognized that he would have to take charge of his life to get a home of his own, financial independence, and a committed lover. The transition, which fell far short of a transformation, had begun.

With some success, I encouraged him to get fresh air, rest and exercise, and exchange ideas with us. I urged him to attend career-counseling sessions, and have a test for HIV plus personal counseling—suggestions he angrily refused. (He did let us pay his dentist for teeth cleaning.) When I invited him to go jogging, he literally ran away from me—clear out of sight—and I didn't see him again till I got back home. And I didn't want him to take our car out at night, then come back in the small hours with some degree of substance impairment—or not come back at all. Moreover, his mother couldn't rest comfortably till he got back. He didn't let on that he'd written any poetry since high school, and generally didn't want to talk about either his past or future. Our best moments were celebrating Thanksgiving in Fayette with some faculty members he liked and seeing an art exhibition at the college plus a restored Victorian home, helping him get a drivers license, playing perquackey, and dining out in Columbia.

Rob was piqued that I bought a ticket to have him, his bags and packs come home by bus rather than by plane. (He left from the New York Port Authority, slept on the bus, and arrived two miles from our house in early evening after a 26-hour trip. We crammed his gear into our car. The bus cost about one fourth taxi and air fares, and there was no problem with the luggage.) He then filled his journal with self-blame for scheduling so long a time in Columbia where he was bored and irritated.

Although he knew he shouldn't spend money on nightlife, Rob resented the fact that I didn't turn over the car at first. He couldn't bear listening to my suggestions for the type jobs he might hold that wouldn't preclude doing some acting. "I DO NOT WANT TO BE A BROADCASTER!," Rob wrote. "He doesn't get it. But do I?"

So he started spending money frivolously during his Texas visit. Back in Columbia, he did drugs furtively in our house, got into the bar scene and paid for some reverse hooking. On the positive side, he did a lot of reading at home and cut his cigarette use by 75 percent. (He dressed "punk" and didn't shave for days. When he went outside our house to smoke, a neighbor phoned that there was a threatening person in our yard.)

Carol was on vacation from her position as library director for the Thanksgiving weekend and we tried to improve communications with Rob. Here's his assessment of why we failed:

> I love my parents, but sometimes they drive me crazy. I think they understand. I kind of wish I could be more open with them—or something. I sometimes feel like they expect something from me. I don't know. Sometimes when I'm with them I feel like I'm under a magnifying glass. I hate that feeling. Do they think I'm not being open enough? Dad referred to me at one point as being a recluse. I guess that is kind of true. I am a loner. I feel as though I'm becoming more of a loner everyday. I don't know how to express myself—or I just don't want to—or I'm afraid—or all of the above.
> I'm craving contact with people my own age. I'm scared, scared, SCARED about heading back to L.A.

In the final days at home, Rob resolved to pursue a relationship—however hopeless—with the Californian and to lead a different, more positive life. When an actress from "Making Porn" wouldn't take him in, he was offered a pad by his college room mate—who had been too tender hearted to euthanize his cats. After she drove him from the L.A. airport on December 4, they stopped at a convenience store. "Good to have a slurpee," he wrote. "Good to see my girls."

During his first week, Rob got together with the aloof Californian, met a dealer who gave him free crystal, and had random sex—triggering a personal record of six orgasms in 12 hours. As for acting or jobs, "I haven't done a Goddamn productive thing since I got here. WHAT THE FUCK IS WRONG WITH ME?"

Rob eventually had sex with the Californian about whom he fantasized constantly. But his idol had so many other friends, and told Rob that he required suitors for a permanent relationship to be over 30, with a job and a credit card. Rob put out a few job applications and perhaps pictures and an acting resume. Craving stability and independence, he complained that he was bored, lonely, and afraid. His evolution into a loner reached the point of no longer desiring a committed lover. He now wanted a pad by himself, a job and a car. (Several of his 1997 and 1998 poems dwell on needing a car.)

When he begged me for a car, I said that a job to justify it came first. (I even mentioned that he could have raised the necessary cash by part-time work while touring.) To the argument that a car was essential for auditions, I said that I would pay for taxis to supplement the buses, that cast members might well take him at least part of the way home. (Ironically we sent him a book about making your way in Hollywood for Christmas that said one needed a car.)

Rob drifted back into getting stoned and tried hooking—at first unsuccessfully. Struggling to achieve a positive self-image, he wrote, "I must totally love myself before I try to give love to someone else." (He would have sporadic doubts about the morality of hooking and speculate about regaining his purity.)

In January, 1997 he got $100, a frolic in a hot tub and a ride home from his first L.A. hooking client. (He had about $5.00 to his name at the time.) That same day, he spoke of attending poetry readings and perhaps publishing poems. Three weeks later he auditioned for a mock-documentary film about Elvis sightings. Applicants had to present their own stories. Rob related how Elvis, serving as an enforcement officer, busted him for growing pot. (The film-maker did not employ Rob.)

In late January, he was disturbed that the Californian's New York lover was coming to visit and that the pair would take a trip to Hawaii. His hooking, which was now profitable, was disrupted by a case of "crabs." "HOW HOW HOW HOW CAN I GET MY LIFE IN ORDER???" The short-term answer was free medicine from the STD Clinic at the Gay and Lesbian Community Center.

Things really changed in February. Aided by a kind word from a former colleague at Berlin, he was hired by a sex club. (He called the job, which apparently required no sex with the clients, "legitimate." He did have to "clean up cum," but it was mostly desk, front window and clerical duties. Perhaps as a customer, however, client lovers sucked his dick there.) He continued hooking in his spare time. Shortly thereafter he got his own apartment—no furniture but he was "very happy to be alone." (He even professed indifference to the Californian who had obsessed him for so long.) He told us that he was working in a bar. We were pleased that he had a job and an apartment (After all, I kept saying, it took him time to get established in Fayette, college, and Chicago.)

Reaching his materialistic goals except for a car must have inspired his poetic urges. "Musing on Life and Home" describes his early days in his apartment and the moral implications of the occupations that made it possible. "Wary" was inspired by a youngster he met at the club. "Acne and Madness" was written when his skin, especially his neck, was broken out. (Rob's clients didn't seem repulsed by the acne, but his self-esteem may have suffered greatly.) In "Envy, Paranoia, and a Promise" he anticipates how he will operate his future car.

Love, however, is the dominant theme of this section despite the humorous poem, "Bureaucracy." "Saugatuck" was a reliving of certain experiences with his former committed partner in Chicago. (As we shall see, the Stevie Smith poem, "Not Waving but Drowning" that he recommended in "Saugatuck," expressed Rob's conception of his place in the world.) Weeks later, in April, the committed partner split from his lover, and Rob wondered about resuming that relationship. "Dressing Before a Cubist Mirror," was a later outreach to his former partner.

While continuing to write his lovelorn laments into the late summer, Rob began an outcast's critique of his society in April. During May, he read "Breaking the Surface," "Fanfaronade," and "Saugatuck" at a coffee house— "the best thing that I have done in a very long time." Following at least one more reading session, he read the first third of "Learning to Howl in Hollywood" at the end of June, and planned two more sessions to complete his "dream poem.". He was delighted when the hostess invited him to appear in a special Saturday night show in July.

LEARNING TO HOWL IN HOLLYWOOD*
(4-12//97)

I.

I am a whisper wrapped
In denim and black leather
Standing on a corner
In this one-horse town
Of repaved cement dreams.
(It didn't take me long to learn
That the one horse is quite stubborn
And must be dragged to its destination
By several million cars.)
I am waiting for a bus again.
Across the boulevard that is called Hollywood
The hombres and the saucy senoritas stream
Into the Guatelinda Nightclub.
"I Donde Se Hacen Amigos!"
The bill board screams.
(Just what the Hell do those words mean?
I am so sorry, Mrs. Burke,
But high school Spanish was millenia ago.
I think I can interpret
"Cuchi Cuchi Salsotec.")
Of course, from where I stand
I have no way of knowing,
But I have an intuition
That these boys smell really clean.
I am quite certain
That these boys still live at home.
I have no doubt
That before they left sus casas
Their mothers roused themselves
From hurculonian (sic) armchairs;
Tore themselves from soaps,
Talk shows, game shows;
Needlessly smoothed their sons'
Gel-laquered, perfect hair;
And told them to have fun.

I am also sure
That these mothers would clutch their rosaries
And kneel in fervent prayer
If they could see the short, short skirts
And hooker heels worn by the girls
Their ninos covet.
I want to yell across the great abyss
The city planners call a street
And ask those buoyant Latin lads
When and how I left their ranks.
(True I was neither straight nor Spanish
But I was once a boy.)
I find myself in a corner on this corner
Caught in some dead-panned limbo.
I am absolutely not a man.
I am absolutely not a boy.
How and when did I become so ancient?
(I grow old; I grow old.
I shall wear my trousers clean, God willing.)
There are so many questions that I want to shout
To those unsuspecting, dance-floor-destined strangers;
But I have inconveniently just misplaced my voice
And my bus has just arrived.

II.

I am finally on the bus,
Ass planted on graffitti-festooned seat—
Another set of hieroglyphics I cannot read.
I am finally on the bus
Which is—not at all unexpectedly—
Caught in crosstown traffic.
(Yes, even at this time of night
The going is quite slow.)
My fellow travelling companions and I
Are being treated to a special screening
(Are those bus windows or movie screens?
You can never tell these days.)
Of yet another scene of some poor rube
Pimping away his promised fifteen famous minutes.

On a corner, outside some bar,
This man—his face erased from view
By a blinding camera-mounted spotlight—
Is being captured for Eternity's collection of souls.
This man is trapped in the cold steel of infamy's bright glare
And we cannot tell if he is of the tourist species
Or just a plain and stupid local.
The bus slowly lurches on—
As always at the most inopportune time—
And we are left to ponder
The outcome of this safari.
Will the hunters have another head
For their well-mounted TV screens
Or will the terrified animal
Chew off his own paw in order to escape?
Another question swallowed with no chaser
By the star-struck L.A. night.
I am finally on the bus;
My boots are in a pile of today's abandoned news.

* The following poems, which are undated, expand the theme of "howling in in Hollywood"—generally protesting a range of life experiences. As the introduction to this unit, the preceding poem appears out of chronological order.

UNPLEASANT NEWS FROM THE FIELD OF MEDICINE

There is a woman in the Windy City
Who, when she wears her hair off of her face,
Eerily resembles the late, great Vivien Leigh.
She called and told me how
One day her right hip
Just up and disappeared.
"It could have been the booze," she says,
"Or it may be a matter for the lawyers."
Either way she is on crutches now—
A temporary state, thank God—

Yet she hobbles through her days
Knowing her other hip may migrate too.

There is a woman fermenting in Milwaukee
Who, come this summer,
Plans to bottle-up her brew
And export it to the West Coast.
(I think there definitely is a market
For what she can produce.)
She called and told me how
She has just been diagnosed
With a serious sleep disorder.
("Oh darling, how exciting," I want to scream,
"I have a sleep disorder too!"
Although mine is self-induced.)
I bite my tongue when I hear
Her's will join her in the counting of the sheep
For the remainder of her life.
I chew the inside of my cheek
When I hear she has to wear this "thing"
To make the problem somewhat better.
I cannot ask her
What the "remainder of her life" means.
I cannot ask her
What that "thing" is.
The smell of hospitals hurtles through the phone lines.

I am the biggest coward in the world.

There is a man hustling his apples
Among the shadows in New York City.
He has a virus coursing through his blood
Chased by denial and by speed.
This man taught me how
To put a value on myself.
This man taught me what
It really means to give.
This man definitely is no angel,
But he does not deserve
To die before his time.

I do not know my generation's greatest minds,
Nor do I think that I would want to;
But I am acquainted
With some of my generation's greatest souls.
The three whose tales I have just told
All fit into that category.
No infirmity of their minds or bodies
Could ever make me love them less,
But I am concerned by their deterioration.

OBIT

Allen Ginsberg died last week.
His ashes now are mingling in a giant urn with
His generation's greatest minds' remains.
I am not well-read enough for eulogies; but
I pray some mischievous, cantankerous
Beat-loving gust of wind
Will steal into the quiet crypt where this urn rests
And whip those great grey genius ashes into
A multiplying horde of frenzied tornado dancers
Who will cha-cha across the land
And coat the throats and lungs
Of the whimpering ones left behind
With the magic soot of long-forgotten rage.

PERSONAL

Lost somewhere on this journey:
My roan-hued voice.
It is liquor-dappled, tobacco-stained,
And will most likely run if cornered.
If you spy it
Snaking through some dark and dirty alley,
Put out a menthol cigarette
Or a saucer of diet coke (or whiskey)
And see if you can tempt it.
Please see if you can catch it.

There is no motivation for any
Mercenary-minded readers of this ad
To return my poor, lost voice
For no reward is being offered.
But then you could not put a price
On my eternal gratitude.
If you should recover it,
And are of the "finders-keeper's" school of thought,
Here is a user's warning for you:
I have been told it is quite powerful,
But I also know, when aiming for notes
Of masculinity or realness,
It can sound quite flat.

FLYING FISHERMAN

"Addressee Unknown: Return to Sender"
Is a most cold shower
After a drunken night
Of eighteen years of friendship.
I have friends I cannot find.
They are scratched-out phone numbers
And unopened, returned letters.
All is lost, Sayonara, "Gone With the Wind."

I have a dream that is bus-free.
I have a fantasy that I can fly—
That I can soar—
That I am one with the mist—
That I am perpendicular to the ground.
In my vision, I take to the air in a night
Without a star to be found.
Yet my eyesight—fore and hind—is twenty-twenty.
I cross the land, a giant net trailing in my wake.
It is a net made of the strongest fiber known to man.
(What that is, I do not know.
I must research this dream.)
I must scoop up every person
Who has ever touched my soul.

I will hook them from the fishbowls of their lives;
I will trap them halfway in their journeys back upstream.
("Baby," I will tell them,
"There'll be later times to spawn.")
I will net them in schools;
I will hunt and catch the Great White Whales.
I will not believe the myth of anyone's elusiveness.

Once my black night's catch is all collected,
I transport us to the deepest canyon on this earth
And there we lowly learn to howl.
We will build a fire and we will learn to howl.
Why a canyon? you may ask.
Well, because quite frankly
We are not ready for the mountain tops.
And besides—what this dream
Lacks in research, it makes up for in grandiosity—
When we are prepared, and only then,
That canyon will become a bull horn;
That canyon will become a megaphone
And it will trumpet our howlings
Out into this staid, dead world
With more intensity and reverb
Than any cliched, mountain-top singing could produce.

There is a man I loved for four long years
(Truth be told, and why not,
I still love him even now)
Who has, for reasons mysterious to me,
Let all his atoms vaporize.
He exists now only in the form of
A woman's electronic voice.
This stacatto, computer-generated bitch
Has only had the power,
Or the gumption, or the will,
To learn one line of script
Delivered by the Production Company of Life:
"The number you have reached
Is not in service at this time.
No further information is available."

Her banal intonations provide little hope
Of any dramatic (or comedic) developments,
Yet I must give her credit for her words—
Does she even know that is what these sounds are called—
Fit quite nicely into the rhythmic structure of this story.
If that is all that I can get these days,
Then I will gladly take it.

I spent this morning on my floor,
Eyes locked with the ceiling's taunting stare,
And realized that I have not one clue
As to who is really lost.
Is it me, or friends I cannot find?

THE LIST IS ENDLESS, BUT HERE'S A START

We will build a fire
And we will learn to howl.
We will howl simply for the joy received
From listening to the sound.
We will howl for missing friends
And hangers-on we cannot shake.
We will howl for fathers
Whose love we cannot fathom.
And mothers who are afraid to move.
We will howl for dreams that did not come true
And for dreams that did, and sucked.
We will howl because we don't care for politics.
We will howl because we don't give a fuck about
Economics—we only want children to get a proper
Education and for the arts to be well funded.
We will howl for diseases and for famines.
We will howl for shaky hips
And sleepless, tortured breath.
We will howl for sisters who have too many babies
And for brothers who raise their children wrong.
We will howl because Lauren Bacall did not win
The Oscar.

We will howl because we are horny.
We will howl because we are lost
And looking for our pack.
We will howl for the knowledge gained
By bathing in the echo.
We will howl because we are tired.
We will howl because nobody believes in us.
We will howl because once, in a moment's weakness.
We believed the hype.
We will howl because we are glorious
And, baby, we know that we are stars.
We will howl because we are different.
We will howl because Belinda Carlisle left L.A.
We will howl for the joy of the mundane
And the banality of the exalted.
We will howl because we have been sleeping
On floors for far too long.
We will howl because the mirrors are not changing,
But our impressions are.
We will howl for poets who have just died
And for poets who have not yet been born.
We will howl because there will always be a reason to.

AYE-YI-YI-YI

The bus has finally palmed me off
To the fertile hills of Silver Lake
Where I stomp heavy in my big, black boots,
Manipulating my walk for a maximum
Of clang and jangle
From the buckles on my biker jacket.
The palm trees are not impressed
By my attempts to break the peace.
The houses are too tired to yawn in disdain.
Their ennui-shaded windows are expressionless.
The guard dogs are not alarmed—
They all have learned my shape and scent.
They follow me behind chain-link fences
Until I have passed their yards

Merely out of respect for their unseen masters.
I only manage to get a rise from
The Bitter dust sleeping on the undulating sidewalks.

"Get a car you loser," the dust motes hiss,
And leave us to our beauty rest.
"We must be ready for our sunrise-scheduled close-ups."

I am looking for a nightclub I can call my own.
I am looking for a sign—in a language I can read.
I am searching for members of my tribe.
I am hunting for my voice.
I am searching for the cure for every cancer.
I am looking for my lost reflections.

I probably should have stayed at home.
Yet here I am gliding through the molecules.
Slipping between tree and post—
Sliding between post and fence—
Sidestepping over-hanging limbs,
I am moving toward the open, lighted hills ahead.

HOORAY FOR HOLLYWOOD

I am becoming the person
I swore I'd never be.
I am really becoming a person
Who really, really wants to be a star.
I am using my connections;
I am constantly dropping names.
I am checking out the cost of selling out.
I am becoming the whore
I've only dreamed of being.

THERAPY OR ART

There are couches here
But I'm on stage.
I'm telling you my darkest secrets,

Yet—though you probably should be—
You're not getting paid.
When it's all over, I feel great.
But how are you?

ANGST '97
(OR HAS MY NEIGHBORHOOD BECOME TOO TRENDY?)

Under strains of modern jazz,
They yell across the table.
They are not angry,
They are just trying to be heard.
Meanwhile, Barbie—against her will—
Is hanging deconstructed on the cafe wall.

She is afraid of being left
Out of her familial loop;
She worries some relative will die
Or be promoted (or perhaps both).
And no one will deem to tell her.
He worries about the price of love in Silverlake.
They both hate their jobs
And do not know what the Hell
They are doing with their lives.
She wonders if Joan Cusak can get a film
Without her brother being in it.
He thinks, "What about 'Toys'—
John Cusak was not in that, was he?"
They have just seen "Grosse Point Blank."
They both skipped their ten-year reunions.
He thinks she is looking thinner than last week.

She thinks he still needs a haircut.
She has no cash on hand.
He spends his money foolishly.
She says the coffee is too bitter.
He thinks Barbie shooting up
Is somehow inappropriate—even as social commentary.

He has forgotten momentarily
That it is all just art.
He fears he is growing puritanical.
She fears he is a slut.
She talks about future vacations.
He talks about past lives.
She wants to be the fly in someone's ointment.
He plans of later getting laid.
She says she wants to get a dog;
He knows he needs new socks.
He wonders why all the men he meets
Are at least five years older than they look;
She reminisces of a room filled with nothing but
Straight men who don't give a shit about Prada or Versace.
He wants to learn where he can find forgiveness
And what the going rate is.
She wants a bar where there is a gin and tonic waiting
As soon as she walks in.
He is concerned that he is smoking
In a room where there's a baby.
They are angry not at each other, but at the world.
Unfortunately, no one is listening.

Under strains of modern jazz
A baby sits on his mother's lap
While his father plays the xylophone
With the combo on the stage.
To his right, there are two flesh-toned shapes
With flailing arms and mouths.
A noxious odor creeps through the air,
But basically the baby is serene.

BEDROOM

This dream, my dream—
Like all great dreams—
Is full of morphing landscapes
And cast with actors
Who can change their faces at will.

We will build a fire
And we will slowly learn to howl.
Metaphorically, we will fuck.
For a howl is born through fornication—
A howl is born through the union of two souls.
I cannot howl in a vacuum.
I cannot howl if I have never loved you—
If I have never lost you.
I cannot howl if you have never made me mad,
Made me laugh.

We must forget someone else's intended purpose
For our bodies and our souls.
We must forget biology and preference.
We must find radical new ways
In which to impregnate each other.
We will find a way
To bring each other's soul to orgasm.

I will give you two eyes.
I will peel back each onion layer of my skin
So you can see my soul.
I will give you tissues
If that onion makes you cry.

I will warn you too
That I am a wayward, wanton wench.
Yea, each of my baby howls
Was fathered by a different man;
But I know each of their daddy's names.
I was married to them all.
My howls, they are not bastards.

In the bedroom, we must pick teams;
But—don't worry—this isn't eighth-grade gym.
We will all play on both sides.
We will all be picked first.
When not on the home team
Of howl-impregnated beings,

We must all be prepared
To go to bat for the midwives
To put our howl-bearing experience to use
For the ones in present labor.

Just breathe and push.
Just squeeze my hand
As tightly as you must—
You can turn my bones to powder.

I must tattoo on my bones
The feeling that I feel
Waking on the floor
Tangled in the flowered sheets
Loaned to me by a pretty, perky girl
With whom I shared a room or two.
(Don't worry; it isn't what you think.)
I must remember how it feels
To wake up twisted with the aching
Of last night's work and to see
First thing another roach
Scurrying across the carpet,
Through a sunbeam home-bound to digest
Its stolen morning feast
Because someday when I am famous
I will sleep under Italian sheets
Of a stratospheric thread-count
In a bed the size of Italy
And my battles with the roaches
Will be the words of history.
If you skip that chapter in your school books,
Let me clue you in: the roaches won.

A PRAYER, IF YOU PLEASE

I pray you understand
This poem-dream's shifting metaphors.
I hope you are not thinking,
"What the Hell is that fag talking about?

> Howling fish fucking in the Grand Canyon!
> I just don't get it.
> What happened to the Spanish boy on the bus?"
> I am not questioning your intelligence
> But my ability to communicate.

July was a hectic month for Rob. Another woman with whom he had roomed for two years of college moved to L.A.—making a stop with her van to pick up his goods in Columbia. When she moved to her own apartment, months later, Rob was gratified.

He was placed in training for a position as assistant manager at the sex club, which created some competition with another employee. When we offered to fly him to Waco for a family reunion and a chance to see his cousin, he told the manager and other employees that his grandfather had died and he was going to the funeral. This lie caused him distress because of his "Catholic school girl" belief that liars are punished in some way. He wrote "The Molting Moon" and "Heartbreak" for someone in Waco he hoped to console following a terminated relationship.

Preceding the Waco trip (late July-early August), I sent Rob a letter asking him to confer with me regarding his future and discuss plans for me to assist him in getting a car. He attended the family dinners, but generally socialized exclusively with his age group. When I thought the time was right, I asked him whether he would like to have a talk. He smiled kindly and said, "No." (My letter was still on his bureau when I arrived in L.A after his hospitalization.)

"Our Last Night" was the longest love poem Rob wrote for the Californian, who was also the subject of "To My Horse." Like a soap-opera hero, however, the Californian was not written out of the drama. While drunk, the two had clashed; but the matter was soon patched over. And Rob remained a friend, but not a favorite, till the end of his life.

The poetry in this section ends with Rob's lament for the death of Princess Diana in late August, 1997—depriving him of yet another love object. For his Christmas gift, I commissioned a small acrylic depicting a spirit riding a spectral horse away from a funeral-burial scene toward lilies which became trumpets sounding victory. (There are several candles, two images of Diana and many more symbols.) Rob hung it on his apartment wall, where I repossessed it after his death along with several of his newspapers that recorded Diana's story. One news photo showing triumphant lilies touched me deeply.

The first four sections of Rob's poetic autobiography end with his moving on to another location and a different way of life. This time he stayed put in L.A., but he had renounced the goal of a life partner and lived alone. And he downgraded his lifelong dream of becoming a successful actor and movie star. Now he wanted to write "like Isak Dinesin at the end of Out of Africa." "Good-bye end of 'Making Porn.' Good-bye New York.... I want to leave a mark here in L.A.—a mark other than the skid marks of another dreamer crashing into a palm tree blinded by the shadow of the Hollywood sign."

PHOTOS

Rooms come back.
Entire days, single moments
All come flooding back
As I look at the old pictures—
The pictures that remind me
How much I loved you.
I thought I had forgotten,
Or buried that love beyond recovery;
But it's still there.
I've got some pictures that'd you'd die
If you knew I had them.
I hope you've got some—
Some pictures of me that make you smile—
Some pictures of me
That nobody else has ever seen.
I hope some rooms come flooding over you
And some single moments too.

SORRY

I've lost a lot of time in a bottle,
Time that will never be returned.
What happened to those moments
After the smiling photo of me
With cocktail in my hand was taken?

SOME QUESTIONS FOR YOU

What's the line between honest and needy?
Where's the line between vulnerable and pathetic?
How much am I allowed
To tell you that I love you?
How long am I supposed to think
Before I say those words?
I don't want to be stupid.
I don't want to be an ass;
But there are moments I can't let go.

Am I repeating myself?
Are these words falling on
Deaf ears and mocking eyes?

FINALLY

After hours of self-abuse.
I decided to forgive myself
And enjoy the rest of the day.
I got stoned
And followed the sun around the porch.

JONESING FOR YOU

I've mainlined your touch
With my vivid, addictive
Obsessive-compulsive imagination.
I've turned your body into lines
And snorted you up until my nose bled,
And I couldn't sleep for days.
I don't want to sound crass,
But I've toked deeply on your joint—
Got so high I couldn't move.
Do you come in pill form?
I've gone to other dealers,
But your stuff is the best.
I need, I want, I lie dying—
Writhing in the sun.
I'm just another casualty—
Just another boy
Who couldn't just say no.

ANYTHING FOR YOU

Baby, I will rock you,
I will hold you,
I will fold you,
I will roll you.

I will carry all the bags
On any trip you charter.
Inside your bulk, behind your gaze
Is that little boy looking out amazed
That anyone could be so damned subservient.
Well, I used to wonder too
How I could forfeit my will to you;
But, baby, maybe I was wrong.
Maybe I'm the one who's strong.
With all your wisdom, and all your grace,
Do you look at me and see nothing but a face
Of youthful desperation?
Maybe in my quiet way
I've picked up all the slack
And found a strength I thought I lacked.
Giving isn't weak.
(I know you never said it was.)
And loving isn't easy.
(I know I'm preaching to the converted.)
But when distant thunder nears
I will cover up your ears.
I will give you anything you need
And be replenished by that deed.

WARNING

Dude,
Do not fall in love with me.
My hair's falling out—
My life's a mess—
Ain't got no job—
Ain't got no car.
It's fucking LA, man
And I ain't got a car.
What are you thinking?
Do not fall in love with me.

SHE KNEW

She sat, and sighed and smoked
When she learned of what her daddy did.
She felt nothing when she heard the news.
The words made no impression.
She was an iceberg floating
In the ice-black ocean.
She was confident in her solitary frigidity.
The kitchen floor must be a mess
Where her daddy smashed her momma's
Head into the linoleum with the iron skillet—
That same iron skillet that had dumped
Greasy bacon onto her plate
On special mornings for years and years.
For years and years, she had often thought
Her daddy would just run her momma over
With the shit-brown Ford—
Anything to shut that woman up,
Anything to blast her balls and chains to Hell.
She wondered if her daddy enjoyed the deed.
Did it happen in slow motion?
Did he savor the symphony of sounds
Created by the collision of skillet meeting skull?
Did goosebumps march up and down his arms
During the overture of clangs and breaking bones?
Were her momma's blood and her daddy's sweat
Swimming round in pools together
During the final encore
Of skillet, brains and floor?
She wondered as she sat and smoked
How many moments in his life
Did her daddy regret.
She knew she'd tell the judge and jury
To have mercy on a poor, old man.
She knew she'd call him every Sunday,
And smoke, and listen to his week.
She knew she wouldn't care that much
When he died too.
She lit another cigarette

And headed to the kitchen
To make her dinner.

JUNIOR

I think your grandma would have beat you blue
If she knew the things you said to me.
Your grandma didn't raise you to be that way.
Maybe your grandpa would have laughed
At the things you did and said; but not her.
She taught you to respect the differences in people.
Who the Hell were you
To point and call me, "Faggot?"
Your grandma would've wondered
The same thing too—If she knew.

SOME OTHER THINGS YOU SHOULD KNOW

Faye Morrison doesn't believe in make-up
She knows there is more power in her wrinkles
And the pallor of her skin than in the
Rosy cheeks some of her friends adopt.
Faye Morrison recycles clothes.
She loves the dress that once belonged
To her dead mother's sister—her dead aunt.
Faye Morrison always carries clean kleenex
In her pocketbook—just in case.

FANFARONADE

I was an actor.
And one day I had a brilliant idea.
While sitting in poverty—
While sitting
With nine dollars to my name,
While facing
The prospect of hooking again—

This is the brilliant idea
That I had:
If I can't be an actor,
Then I'll be a poet.
I'll publish the poems I write in my journal—
A brilliant idea—
The most logical, most natural next step.
How insane to go back to school
To study to be a doctor or lawyer.
How inane to have a trade.
I am an artist.
I will jump from one sinking ship to another.
How relieved the girl
On whose couch I've been crashing
Will be
When she learns of my plan.
The life of a poet
Is so much more practical
Than that of an actor.
I won't need a car to go to auditions.
I'll simply sit home and write poems
To send to chic magazines
Which will publish them with great fanfare
Before they are gathered together
In slim, leather-bound volumes
Which will sell like Miatas
To cool, witty people
Who admire my talent.
I'll be rich.
I'll be a gay, optimistic Sylvia Plath—
A T.S. Eliot for the nineties.
The Broadway musicals based on my poems
Will be called "Faggots" and "Whores."
Live the magic again.
I'll be knighted, and Madonna will star
In the screen adaptation of one of my shows—
Either "Faggots" or "Whores"—
In the role she was destined to play.

KATIE

Katie's got her eye on a fly
That's been buzzing by.
Katie is focused; Katie doesn't hear
Jane's addiction on the stereo.
Katie doesn't see my addictions
Sitting 'round me on the porch.

ETERNAL SPRINGS HOPE

I hope somebody sees
Something in me tonight.
I hope my investment pays off.
I hope the bus comes soon
Because I so hate
Standing here stoned
Clutching my last dimes and nickels
With which I will pay
The fare on said bus.
I hope I can be something
For someone tonight.
I hope someone can put a price
On what I have to give.
I hope no one can see
That I've worn these same jeans
Three times without washing them.
I hope the bus isn't crowded.
I hope the bar is.

NIGHTMARE BY THE SHANGRI LA'S

It happened just like
It would have in a movie.
You know how the camera would pan
To an apartment in the hills.
Then it would zoom
Into the bedroom
And there I'd be.

Well, there I was with my man
Making love to me.
Oh, Byron, Don't stop! Don't stop!
Byron always wondered how
I could afford this apartment.
This was the night
Byron would finally find out.
Cause my sugar daddy
Came banging upon the door.
He kicked it in and the moonlight
Came spilling in behind him.
And we could see the revolver
He held in his hand.
Both of them screamed at the same time,
"How could you do this to me?"
I sat and pondered that question
As Byron ran naked to the doorway.
He slammed my sugar daddy
Into the courtyard
Where they tussled till the gunshot
Pierced the California night sky.
I screamed, and knowing what I would see
If I ran out into the courtyard,
I stayed kneeling in prayer on my bed.
"Byron! Please don't leave me!"
The puddle of blood that I knew
He must be lying in told me
That no one would be hearing my prayers.
I ran and locked the front door.
My sugar daddy was stranded
And he did roar and roar.
I ran into the bathroom
And locked that door too.
And went fumbling through the vanity drawer.
I found my speed
And I poured out a great big line.
The speed bumps were something
Neither of those men knew about.
I took that rail
And as my head came flying up

I saw my reflection.
Every pore was expanding
Into the shape of the head
Of a man I had used.
Tiny little men in suits
Were drowning in the black pools
Flooding round my eyes.
Then I started to pick
And tried to scratch
My way back to purity.
I finally forced myself to stop
And consider the situation
That was at hand.
I had a lover dying out by the fountain
And a deranged sugar daddy
Storming around my courtyard.
I called 911
And said I needed help.
Perhaps an understatement,
But nonetheless I went
Running out into the courtyard
Where I was surprised by the silence.
My sugar daddy was long gone
And Byron lay oh so still.
The palm trees were mournful and solemn
And Byron's blood had begun to dry.
On a flagstone lay the guilty revolver—
A gun that I suddenly remembered
Having used, definitely unloaded—
In a sex scene in my sugar daddy's house.
He was such a kinky man.
My fingerprints were all over that gun.
I said, "I'm sorry, Byron," as the sirens stopped
At the front of my building.
"I'm sorry that there's nowhere for us to run."

BUREAUCRACY

Who is in charge around here?
To whom may I voice a complaint?
This is not the life I thought I'd be living.
I thought by now my skin would be different.
I thought by now the scene would have changed.
To whom may I rant?
To whom may I rave?
Where are they doling out
The life that I crave?
Nobody cares? Well, that's no surprise.
May I borrow your pen to gouge out my eyes?
I know I'm melodramatic,
But what can I do?
I know that you're busy
So just point me to
The department responsible for
Making sure I don't commit
The same mistakes again and again.
There is no such department?
Where the hell is my tax money going?
Who is your supervisor?
Who should I be blowing?
I will not calm down.
I will not lower my voice.
Do you think I'd be standing here
If I had any other choice?
Go back to what you were doing.
Please take that phone call.
I'll leave you alone
And smash my head into the wall.
I have one final request—
If it's not too much trouble—
Give me the forms to get rid of this life.
No, I don't mind filling them out in double.

TO MY HORSE

I've been bucked by you before
So it came as no surprise
To find myself face down in dust
My booted foot tangled in your stirrup
As you dragged me cross the desert floor
Like I was a silent movie comic cowboy.
Where's a camera when you really need one?
Unfortunately not even filmed reminders
Of the lessons I have learned from riding in your saddle
Would keep me from picking up the reins again.
I'm tenacious even when I'm wrong,
And I have no one but me to blame
For the bruises and the scars.
I'll be the first to say I'm pretty green,
Yet with one glance I knew you'd throw me
Your stare said, "More than once."
I could have picked another steed,
But I knew you'd make a man of me—
Or at least I'd die a legend.
I may never tame you—
In truth I love your wildness—
But you will never break my will to try.

NO NAMES HAVE BEEN CHANGED BECAUSE NO ONE IS INNOCENT

I've been having sex with men
Who fit their names.
A___ drove a black Cadillac
And made me take my boots off
Before entering his apartment.
His carpet was shit brown
But it was new.
W____ fell in love too fast
And called me "baby"
And derivatives of my given name
Used only by my family,

And even then not very often.
R____ was a narcissistic con man
Who kissed his reflection as I stroked his thigh.
He brought two leather jackets to the hotel room
He had rented for our special night
Which lasted an hour to the minute.
He wanted my opinion
Of which he looked best in.
Since it was his dime,
I told him both were really "hot."
I wonder if I should be concerned
Since his name is the same as mine.
Friday night I met a man named Ralph.
I haven't slept with him yet,
But I'm sure he wouldn't break the pattern.

MUSINGS ON LIFE AND HOME

My bed is on the floor these days,
But I'm lucky to have sheets.
In my gratitude, I forgive the fact
That they are of a floral, pink nature.
They were lent to me
By a girl named Ginny
Who saw me naked several times a week
For lo' unto a year.
(And unless you know me,
It wasn't what you think.)
Every day is a picnic
As I sit cross-legged and take my meals
In my cotton flower garden
In the middle of L.A.
Almost every new thing I have
Was bought with money that I earned.
Some may say my wages were ill-gained,
But I held a gun to no one's head.
(Perhaps my crime was worse.
I held illusions to my victims' hearts.)
My clothes are clean and hanging neatly—

All shades of blue and green.
The colors are perfect metaphors for me—
Sad and jealous,
And in diametric opposition—
Sea and sky and freshness.
The sinks occasionally drip,
And across the counters I see roaches slip,
But I'm finally living in a world
That I'm creating.
As sleep slides over me,
I count my blessings and ask forgiveness—
From whom I am not sure—
For whatever sins I may have committed.
Pioneers must be expected to err from time to time.
And every morning as I rise
(Well, yes, sometimes it is after noon)
I resume my quest for the meaning of right and wrong.

COUNTING BACK TO ONE

I've had my last bad day;
I've had my last regret.
I'm counting back to one.
I'm through with other voices;
I'm through with buying lies.
I'm counting back to one.
I'll purify myself by walking
Through as many fires as I can.
I'm counting back to one.
I realize I may never be done.

I've smiled my last fake smile;
I've told my last white lie.
I'm counting back to one.
I'll never bit my tongue again;
I'll never hold my breath for you again.
I'm counting back to one.
I'll forgive myself by becoming
The only judge of my own actions.

I'm counting back to one.
I realize I may never be done.

WARY

You say you think
I'm the cutest boy here.
I say you better have
Your eyesight checked;
You'd better stick around.
This lighting is quite good
And the night—unlike me—is young.
You have the most gorgeous smile
I have ever seen,
But I'm suspicious of your words.
Are you on drugs?
Perhaps the explanation is
That you've missed your medication.

ENVY, PARANOIA, AND A PROMISE

Oh, if only I had a horn to honk!
The irate yuppie in the black Range Rover
Has no idea what it means to be impatient,
Has no idea what it means to wait.
So the blonde in the Mercedes in front of him
Didn't hit the accelator the nanosecond
The light turned green.
Is that any reason for his rude blaring?
After you have stood at a bus stop in L.A.,
Then I will let you be impatient.
Once you have abandoned all control
Over the timing of your destiny,
Then I will let you be irate.

I have been carless in other cities,
But it is different in Los Angeles.
Here the cars mock me.
The bumpers sneer.

The headlights leer.
I swear the drivers laugh
As they zoom by—
Laugh at my poor pedestrian plight.

When I have a car again,
I will drive with courtesy.
I will drive with modesty.

ACNE AND MADNESS

The voices in his sleep
Tell him to tear his face apart.
"There is something there. Squeeze a little harder.
Pick a little deeper. That something has to go."
He screams, not recalling ever having drifted off.
He panics when he sees the blood on his pillow
And his hands.
Yet he knows from whence it came.
The mirror shows him pores
That twist into the heads
Of every man he has ever used.
Every drug he has ever tried—
And he has tried them all—
Has failed him. None have done the trick.
None have made his face disappear.
When he undresses in front of strangers,
Is it to see how easily they are repulsed
Or how much derision he can stand?
The doctors say that, at his age,
He should let nature take its course.
"Oh, yes," he thinks, "nature has been so fair thus far."
He wonders if there are pit marks
On that thing the doctors call his heart.
He wonders if there are kelloids
On that thing the other doctors call his soul.
He knows that he is much too old for this.
The voices in his sleep
Tell him to tear his face apart.
He obeys.

SAUGATUCK

Sometimes in the summer
I would stumble home from work,
Draped in the grimy cloak of morning,
My head buzzing from cheap spirits,
My head fuzzy with low spirits,
And you would meet me at our front door.
We would kiss,
(Or at least I hope that's what we did),
Grab our baggage and exit out the back.
I'd fall into the jeep.
You would drive and I would sleep,
And when I woke we would be
On the other shore of Lake Michigan.

Sometimes in the summer
We would go to Saugatuck.
Or Suck-N-Fuck as we would fondly call it.

What was the name of that dreary gay resort
In which we stayed? I can't recall, or won't.
I do remember that it had a pool
And that it had a bar.
How we swam—in chlorine and in liquor.
And if the sun was really high,
We'd venture out into the lake
And always be caught off guard by its severe frigidity.
I remember once you warned me not to go too far out.
Oh, my love, you spoke too late.
(I've just discovered Stevie Smith's
"Not Waving But Drowning."
Perhaps I'll send a copy. It could explain so much.)
Going to the lake in truth meant going to the dunes
Where we would claim our very own secluded spot
And make hot, slow love in the hot, quick sand.
(Or at least I hope that's what we did.)
Once as you dozed beneath an August ball of fire
I looked over the dunes,
Across the stretch of platinum sand,

And in the ripples on the surface of the lake
Saw James Mason leaving Judy Garland.
What were we pale Anglo-Saxon-blooded boys thinking
Lying naked in the open summer air?
Perhaps the sunburns exist only in my over-eager memory.
Can you remember ever getting burned?
I know I never got a tan. Alas! Oh, well.

Some times in the summer
We just had to leave Chicago.

The nights in Saugatuck were made for masquerades.
We'd tumble from our cabin shielded from the eyes of God
By a navy, star-encrusted veil to find our perch
Inside the resort's bar. "Oh, barkeep, if you please,
A Jager, a fruity shot (for me), and two beers."
Armed with our standard magic potion
We would drink and pray that we'd connect
To each other and hopefully to someone else.
We were on vacation after all.
In Saugatuck we always closed down the bar.
If a useful stranger had not been discovered by last call,
We would fall back out into the pitch-black night
And wander blitzed through the famous maze of pines
Pushing back the shadows to try to see
The other men hiding from the moonlight.
I remember once we found and made a friend of
A boy with just-pierced nipples.

Saugatuck was the town for finding something different.

If I had been sober (which is like saying,
"If I had been purple") I would have told you.
I didn't want anybody new.
I only wanted you. I only wanted you.
Who decided that was the game
That we would play? And who made the rules?
I am not blaming. I'm just asking.
Regardless of whose idea it was,
The liquor made me play to win.

And even when you had wearied of the chase,
My engines still were always gunning hard.
Please tell me why I couldn't make them stop.
I loved you so much in Saugatuck.
I remember when you took my hand
And told me I was handsome. Somehow
That just was not enough. I lied in Saugatuck.
I disappeared in Saugatuck. I started losing you
In Saugatuck sometime in the summer.

THOUGHTS THAT KEEP ME FROM MY SLEEP

I wonder if the Big One came
And this fragile earth quaked and rolled
And swallowed me whole,
Would I be spat back out
Because I tasted bad?

I wonder if I offered my soul down to Lucifer,
Would he tell me I should keep it
Because tattered, ratty souls like mine
Are a dime a dozen?

(n.t.; n.d)

Feel like I am playing fort again
At the ripe old age of twenty-eight,
Peering over cardboard walls
Through camouflage of green haze
Down upon my enemies—the world.
Alone in my fort up in the trees
Surrounded by the treasures
Dragged from home—
Still in the backyard; but still quite far
From mother ideal.

I am in the same fort.
It is the same tree;

But now I'm not afraid
To let you see the wormholes.
Come on and climb me, baby!
Let me tell you the one
About when the worms ate
Right through my heart.
If you cannot handle the scarred-up bark,
Just wait till you see the mangled pulp
Of what was once my heart.

Come fuck with me.

Come throw your hardest snowball
In the deadest dead of winter.

I am in my fort alone.

MISSOURI FEVER

I couldn't shake it in Chicago.
It didn't break in N.Y.C.
And when I wake up sweating in L.A.,
I know the reason why:
I've got the Missouri fever
And from it eventually I'll die.

My oldest friend, Ann, and I
Have already decided, sworn
That when we weary of the hunt
For that rascal youth, escape,
We'll retire to a farm
In the grand ol' Show Me State
And plant and harvest naught but weed,
And sing the sunsets to their sleep
In the bosom of the hills
And rock the nights away
With fireflies and stars
From the comfort of our porch.
I've got the Missouri fever
And from it eventually I'll die.

OUR LAST NIGHT
(For __ with love strained through
a sieve of anger, embarrassment,
and remorse)

I am tempted—lying on my floor
Ignoring dirty dishes,
Watching Night make herself comfortable
In my only chair in my only room—
I am tempted to pick up that phone,
Dial, wait for you to answer,
And beg for your forgiveness.

I am tempted—smoking another cigarette,
Kitchen faucet dripping in my mind,
Succumbing to the open arms
Of Night's subtle gardenia perfume
Dabbed behind her ears—
I am tempted to pick up that phone,
Dial, stop breathing till you answer,
And tell you why I do the things I do.

But Night, arms folded, legs crossed
Is shaking her head "No"
To the rhythm of the dripping water.
Through gardenia haze and smoke
I can see the phone receiver is quite content,
Cradled in its base, and does not wish to be disturbed.
More to the point: I owe you no apologies.

And my explanations would send you off to sleep
Unless, of course, you have just shot up
Another gram of coke, and then...
Well, then, that would be a different story.
Or perhaps not, for when we last met
We were both returning from journeys taken by rail—
Different lines,* exact same destination.

It is no one's fault
That our last night unfolded like a movie

Or that the unseen director
Was a Steven Spielberg wannabe
Who could not decide between remaking
"Jaws" or "Schindler's List,"
And who, in his indecision, made another film
About once-believed-to-be-extinct monsters
Devouring idealistic scientists.

(Night has nodded off.
Movie analogies bore her stiff.)

Without question—,
You make a perfect leading man;
You are Paul Newman and Marlon Brando's
Long lost, well-lit love child—You
Are every gay movie-goer's wet dream.
And me? Me? What about me?
Well I…I am no leading lady.
Gender fuck has never been my cup of tea
And I am much too honest
To think that I could ever pass
As a lady—leading or otherwise.

I…I am the naive friend—
Alright, I'll call a spade a spade—,
I am the stupid friend
Who ignores common sense and scary music
And screamed advice from audience members,
And always goes back into the house
Where the slasher is in the attic
And the psycho is in the basement
And the doors become unopenable
As soon as they are shut.

If our last night was a movie,
And since I say it was,
It must be true—
There are several things
For which I am quite grateful:
The script has mercifully been shredded.

The negatives have all been burned,
And the director is now doing
An all-male version of "Guys and Dolls"
In a community theatre in West Covina.

And though I am relieved
That this film will never see the light of day,
There are some scenes
I will always consider Oscar-worthy.

Running hand in hand through sprinklers—
Suspended briefly in mid-air—
Azure, with the mist, transparent,
We and the water must have landed,
Settled, but I don't remember it;

Lots of bars and lots of drinks—
All the same crowded Jagermeister blur,
You showed me your veins;
I showed you my heart—
I do not believe either one of us
Was particularly impressed;

Holding up a wall
As you washed your wounds
Inflicted during another self-righteous battle
Against yourself and the too-imperfect world;

Standing on a corner
In a light that ignored reality—
Standing on a corner
Having been dismissed by you—
Standing on a corner
Forcing the school of lemmings,
Dress extras chosen for their blandness,
To split and swim around me—
Standing on a corner
Intoxicated and indignant,
My stick arm outstretched,
Rage and bitter fury flowing

From my shoulder to the pointing
Nail-bitten tip of my angry index finger—
Standing on a corner
Milking melodrama,
Telling you not once but twice
That you will never know how much I love you—
Standing on a corner
Seeing Hurt's cousin sitting in your eyes
Feeling oh so right and cruel and childish
And without shame—
Standing on a corner turning;

Another bus, another bus ride,
Another fucking, fucking, goddamn bus ride
To the intersection of darkness and nowhere
Where I found a pay phone,
Dropped a quarter,
And read a poem I had written for you
To your indifferent answering machine.

Flick, flick, flick, flick
Flicker, flick
The film and my memories
Spin and fly
Around the take-up reel.

I am still tempted—
Several evenings since I started writing this:
Sitting at a table outside the Onyx,
Having left home alone;
In my room with the vigilante roaches,
Ignoring the wisdom of gently letting go—
I am still tempted.

* A "line" is a unit of cocaine.

(n.t., 7/7/97)

Glass slippers shatter.
Castles are flammable.

Princesses of poverty
Wed greasy-haired Dukes
Who ride sweaty on old Harleys.

The fleas on my cats
Will not become coachmen.

DRESSING BEFORE A CUBIST MIRROR

If we were hopscotch and I landed
One foot in your square,
Would you recognize me or I you?
I ask because I no longer wear
The clothes of shame you knew.
I have outgrown them all
And thrown them all away.
My robe of envy has unraveled
And will not be replaced.
I am shirts now that you
Have never washed or folded.
On hangers in a walk-in closet
I am blue riots
Spun by polyester spiders
In the long-gone seventies
But bought on Fairfax just last week.
I am metallic Fila—
I glitter turquoise, shimmer athletic
In the label-conscious sun;
I am flowered Western passed-along
Admired by the tourist girls in Akbor
As I embrace their boyfriends' ugly dancing.
If you twist and focus your kaleidoscope
On this western shore,
You might see me slicing Sunset
Wearing nothing but a bathrobe
As I stare down the hate-filled high beams
With the eyes my father loaned me.
If you twist and focus, you might see

Me dreaming of vintage chaps
Like the ones Elvis wore in "Nowhere."
If you twist and focus, you might see
Me in the Hawaiian skirt I'll wear to work tonight.
I will not wear underwear under it.
If you twist and focus, you might see
Me in the boned corset
Sewn from the skin that I wear
When I practice tight-rope walking.
I am marbles now
Waiting for the next collision
To send me hurling, spinning, whirling
Into someone else's pocket.
But in L.A. I lie awake and dream
That you love me still.
What do you wear when you walk Quick Red Irish
Through the slush-snow, blueberry sun of Maine?
What do you wear in the land of L.L. Bean?
Please tell me so I can recognize you when
I land one foot in your square.

THE MOLTING MOON
(FOR...)

It is much harder
When you hear the words from him—
Words that have worn out
The treadmill of your brain,
Words that have made
Your muscles atrophy.
When you hear the words from him
You lose your mind,
You lose your floor,
The hinges all reject the doors,
The frames spit out the doors.
The doors sigh and lean and twist,
And at last fall down and fall
And fall forever, fall forever
Because there is no floor.

You sit on your porch
In your dusty Texas town
And smoke volcanoes and cry earthquakes

And say to yourself
And to whomever is on the phone,
"It is over. It is really over."
You canot ask the molting Moon
What all this is supposed to mean.
Just run into your tear-dewed lawn
And gather up her feathers
And stuff them tight into your pillow,
And try to sleep,
And try to dream.
When you hear the words from him
You lose your strength,
Your windows shatter;
Your windows all explode,
Glass flies into the street.
Your state becomes an ice cube.
You cannot move. You have to watch it melt.
Your horizons set sail on the ice cube's puddle.
Your horizons set and sail away.
Your horizons melt away.
You can cry hurricanes,
And you can smoke tornadoes;

But you cannot ask the molting moon
What all this is supposed to mean.
Just run off your porch
And grab that shedded skin
And make yourself a belt
To hold your spirits up.
Don't notch that belt too tightly though;
Please remember how to breathe.
I will fly down soon
To hold your hand—
To give you both my hands.
You can squeeze them hard,
Just breathe and squeeze,

You can turn my bones to dust.
I will fly down soon
To be with you.
But I have no more answers
Than the molting moon.

HEARTBREAK *

It is heartbreak
Don't tell me you've been robbed;
Don't tell me you feel raped.
Don't cloak your pain in metaphor—
It does not need that false adornment.

* For the same person as the preceding poem.

ANGER CHANGES EARTH AND SKY *

On a highway in the desert
In his brand new Acura,
He turns the median
Into a coke fiend's
Desperate first snort.
His nose is burning in the hot sun,
Reflecting and attacking
From the mirror of the pavement.
He is anxious in his bare feet;
He will not let the pedal rest.
The fire from his engine turns
The desert's sand to glass.
He doesn't have the time
For artistic pretensions.
He doesn't blow and twist and form;
He doesn't use a mold.
He hasn't slept and thinks not once
Of abandoning this piece of master craft,
This piece of shit to the overburdened state.
Let some future scientist explain
The geologic transformation.

The world is orange and the glass bleeds bubbles
As it tries to find a shape.
He will never see it cooled.
The carburetor doesn't give a fuck,
And the battery agrees;
But the steering wheel is not so certain
As it feels his boiling, blistered hands
Closing, circling round its neck.
He wishes he could give the rear-view mirror
A swollen, tightly shut black eye.
He does not want anyone to see
The exhaust of his past.

As he closes in on home,
He is very conscious of the windows.
They are brazen whores, lifting skirts
When an expensive car approaches.
Their legs spread easily;
They do not believe in secrets.
He will send them to a convent
And the mercy of the twisted ruler-nuns.
He will close the gaping holes
With chastity belts of plywood.

In his house, he smashes bottles and decanters;
He takes up golfing with the goblets.
He hauls the shards and jagged bits
Into the yard and hurls them to the Heavens.
They slice the sky, and slash the night,
And replace retiring stars.

* For the same person as the preceding poems.

(n.t., n.d. *)

Dreams throb through car radios,
Out of car windows,
Vibrate in cars idling
Waiting for change.
We buried a queen today.

In the distance down Hollywood
The sun sets into reruns
Ingesting fire/lanes of traffic
While easily birthing more of the same.
We buried the princess today.

I scream on the sidewalk.
Scare innocent families.
I say to the bus doors, "Reality is overrated."
The doors merely yawn and swallow me whole.
We buried a woman today.

*Author revered Princess Diana (d. August, 1997).

VII.

HOMOEROTICISM AND DESPAIR

As he entered the last 10 months of his life, Rob felt the need to make new friends who shared his interests in poetry, movies, music, fashion and antique furniture. But he was so ashamed of his lifestyle that he felt nobody would become his friend because he had so little to offer them.

By the end of summer, he wanted to resume his "stalled" acting career, and made a New Years wish to do so for 1998. He had some unsuccessful auditions the following spring—without a car to get to them although he bemoaned the lack of one repeatedly in his journal. He wrote that he wanted to get back into acting to boost his "self-esteem" (without asking whether acting had boosted it while touring).

Particularly during my initial grieving over his death, I pondered why Rob wouldn't talk to me in Texas about his future and discuss plans for me to get him a car (I was going to give him the one I was driving if he seemed ready to maintain it). Afterward, he referred to me as "Bart" rather than Dad in his journal. Of course, I may have tried to have serious talks when the timing wasn't right. Here's his slant on better communications when he was planning a June, 1998 trip to Missouri to see his consort in the poem "Missouri Fever."

> It would also be good to see my parents. It would, wouldn't it? Oh God. I feel like such a failure, but I do miss my parents, but it is so hard talking to them right, I have to lie, and hide so much, and try to sound optimistic. Ugh. Urgh. I do need to communicate with them more. Maybe if I talk more, tell them more, things will be easier. I don't know.

Regrettably, he never visited Missouri again and kept everything essential about his life and emotional state a complete secret from us.

In late March, Rob quit his job at the sex club after being pressured to work more than four days per week. (The underlying cause was that he hated the very thought of any work besides acting.) His disgust with his life, and self-loathing were intense about then. He wanted to contribute something positive to the world and wondered "how God or fate or whatever could put the dreams I have in my ugly carcass." Improving his body at the gym didn't change the fact that his "foul, horrible skin" covered the muscles.

He did apply unsuccessfully for some jobs, and particularly wished to conduct sales at an antique shop or become a radio announcer. (Pointing to the example of Ronald Reagan, I had long suggested that announcing might lead to acting opportunities.) Although he conducted random sex with the Californian and others, Rob doesn't mention any hooking engagements during his last months. As usual, we helped him financially and I was encouraged that he was both seeking employment and auditioning for plays. He was grateful that we called each week, but we didn't know that he was seriously depressed. (A perceptive friend told him that his declining libido was a classic symptom of depression.)

Saying nothing about the poems he wrote during this period; Rob just entered them in his journal. He reports a few pleasant days, with poetry readings by far the high points. Toward the end of his life, his poetry "dried up" and he lacked new material to present. The homoerotic poems in this section are often passionate, but rather joyless. "Senseless" and the 5/3/98, untitled poem are hymns to despair. But the gloomy "Dizzy on the Dog" ends with an affirmation of human brotherhood. As always when a big change in his life took place, he took stock and set goals.

His concluding journal entry is arguably too personal for publication, and too sensational. But let me tell you what happened to some of the young men who grew up on our block in Fayette while Rob attended school for eight years. (Our street with large trees and mostly large Victorian homes lay one block west of Central Methodist College. Our neighbors were professors, professionals, and successful middle class people.) One lad was smothered while playing in a grain elevator, another died from a mugging while serving in the army; and a third was killed in a car crash. Besides a youth who was institutionalized for substance abuse, a young man just around the corner came home from the West Coast to die of AIDS—seriously speech impaired and deficient in motor functions. Rather than keep the AIDS secret, his mother put his plight on film for showing at the high school and college. She couldn't have enjoyed doing this, and surely hoped that such a graphic portrayal would further the safe-sex or no-sex cause. I have a comparable hope that Rob's last journal entries will have some positive effect.

> Feel like I have hit rock bottom. Life seems so bleak and hopeless....MY HAIR IS FALLING OUT. That is the worst. Could be stress. Please God, let me get my life in order so the horrible stress will go away and my hair will grow back....
> I have such a clear image of the life that I want. I just don't know how to get it. I live in a fantasy world, but why should I have to settle for less?

He was miserable from lethargy, sleeplessness, loneliness, distaste for food, his untidy apartment, neglect of personal hygiene, fear of insanity, death wishes and anger because he could not take care of himself. When the Californian said he should move on to Act II of his life, Rob wasn't quite ready to end Act I. "Am I clinging to dreams that won't come true?"

In a final entry from L.A. County Hospital, Rob started referring to me as "Dad" again as he waited for me to arrive. Thinking correctly that he had AIDS and double pneumonia, he didn't completely despair. His female room mates during college were "God-sends."

> The first time they both came to visit, I just saw them so clearly—how beautiful and wonderful and fabulous they are. I am so blessed. So lucky.
> Regrets. Why did I let this happen? Why didn't I take better care of myself? Why didn't I get tested sooner? How could I have hated myself so much to be so self-destructive?

When one of the women advised him to consider the illness as a new beginning, he wrote:. "Don't know how long this next phase will last, but I want to make the most of it."

THIS IS WHAT I'D SAY IF YOU FELL BACK INTO MY LIFE TONIGHT

All you have to do
Is enjoy the night.
An added bonus would be
To see the sunbeams kiss
Your glowing, happy cheeks—

To see two green eyes
Reaching out to hug the day.
Please don't want to run away
Too quick. I know you'll go.
And I'm not asking you to stay.
Just stand long enough
So I can photograph the air
Between our bodies.
Just stand still long enough
So I can freeze you in my mind.
I'm not asking you to stay.
Because I know you gotta go away.
Just look deep enough into my eyes
To know how much I'll always love you.
Just look deep enough into my eyes
To want me for just one night
(Because I know I can make you want me
For just one night)
Before you have to go away.
I know you have to go away.
Just open up your mouth enough
To tell me you're OK.
Just open up your mouth enough
To let me kiss streams of beer
Into the cavern river of your throat.
I know you'll like that.
I know you gotta go away.
I won't be asking you to stay.
Just stay long enough so that I can slip you tongue.

Just stay long enough so that I can slip
My photo into the wallet of your heart's meaning.
Then go away.
You have to go away.

ANTICIPATION

I am going to give you the loving you need.
I cannot make this bus or time move fast enough.
I cannot wait for you to pin me to the wall
And smother me with kisses.
I cannot wait for your tongue to trace
The contours of my neck.
I need some of that scent
Of which Walt Whitman sang.
Oh baby, lift your arms to Heaven
And give me some of that aroma finer than prayer.
I want to feel you twist my soul
Out through my nipples with your rough-loving hands.
I can't wait for you to subjugate me,
Vindicate me,
Elevate me,
Desecrate me.
I have to get to you before I explode
And my shards of love impale poor, passing strangers.

I'M READY

I'm ready to take that walk again—
To tumble down the aisle again.
Maybe this time I'll get it right.
Maybe this time I'll know
If I'm the bride or groom—
Either way I won't be wearing white.
I'm ready for a body
That is more than just two holes.
I'm ready to hear words
Other than "Great cock."
I'm ready to leave the dark rooms

And the groping, grasping strangers
Standing anxious, heaving, unfulfilled
In puddles of their own making.
I'm ready for sex to have some meaning.
I'm ready for sex with the lights on.
I'm ready to wake up glowing and yet so drained
And tip the sheets from our rode-hard,
Put-away wet bed cum love soak-stained.

I'm ready to do your laundry.
Baby, have you got enough bleach for mine?
I'm ready for my life to go to pots and pans again.
I'm ready to cook your favorite meals.
I'm ready to do the dishes for two.
I'm ready to eat for three.
I'm ready to stop wandering restless, reeling, reckless
And to start wondering hopeful, future-flown.
I'm ready for a honeymoon
In the Vegas of your mind,
Or the Caribbean of your soul,
Or the Paris of your ass.
Fuck it, why make decisions?
I'm ready for the endless cruise around your world.
I'm ready to tuck you in.
And fuck you blind and hard.
And then kiss you softly like a secret,
Turn the lights off, and slip to sleep.

THINGS TO DO BEFORE SOMEDAY

I must take a picture
In the only way I know
Of this family walking down the street.
He is sunburnt, birth-right brown
And guards the street side of the sidewalk.
Grinning, his pearly whites have won
The battle against tobacco stains.
He is wearing a grease-stained,
Brando-worthy tee and khakis

That you won't find at the Gap.
She is a shape that Vogue will never sell.
All short and curves,
She pushes the baby stroller
In her high-black, high-heel shoes
Showing off to anyone who's looking
Her brand new Saturday night dress.
Like her shoes and hair,
The dress is black, but streaked
With lurid, third-world silver threads
That venus-fly trap the dusk-chased California sun.
A bra-strap of 12:03 a.m. blue
Sneaks from an arm-hole
And slithers down her shoulder.
She doesn't care.
(And, by the way, to call it midnight blue
Just wouldn't do that bra-strap justice.)
The woman and the man smile
But do not say a word
As they watch their two older children
Race the road to waiting corner.
I must take a picture of this family
Because someday when I am famous
I will not have to stand and wait for buses
On the edge of Hollywood
And families like this one
Won't be walking through the neighborhood
That I'll live in.

Returning home via Vermont
From a shopping expedition
For inner peace and new tennis shoes,
I stopped on a dime when I saw two men
Seated at an out-door cafe speaking to each other
In voices louder than required
And holding copies of identical, slim books.
(I stooped to pick up that dime.
Money is quite needed now.
Inner peace cost more than I thought—
To say nothing of my Nikes.)

And as I stood, it dawned on me
These two men must be actors
Trying to learn new lines
And practicing their projection.
(I am an actor too, myself, sometimes
So do not assume that deduction came easily to me.)
I stopped and story-boarded on the sidewalk
My course of present action:
It is time, I thought, for some community service;
It is time to do something for my country.
I would walk—no, march—up to their table,
Pull up a chair and demand they hear me out.
Have you seen, I would ask,
The road that you have chosen
And do you know that
The cement was poured by Lucifer?
(Though I am not conventionally religious,
A little fanaticism often comes in handy.)
Let me tell you, I would say, some tales
That will shake you to your senses
And cause your hair to stand on end.
Shut up! I can see quite well
That one of you is bald.
How chic. Now hear me out;
I am trying to save your lives.
Let me tell you of my taste of fame.
True, it was the smallest portion on the menu;
But it was the quality, not size,
That left me so dissatisfied.
Let me tell you how I abandoned
My life and cats not once, but twice,
And traveled across the country
To try to spear that rolling, pea-like
Bit of success.
Let me list the side-dishes I sampled
On my recent journey to off-Broadway:
Ego and stupidity were always plentiful;
But my favorite had to be
Addiction smothered in a thick sauce of escape.
Do you want the recipe?

(n.t., n.d.)

Last night we rolled around
On rumpled sheets and memories
And I looked for the burning halo
I saw circling round your head
The night we first met
But found only hair grown saltier
And I tried drowning in your eyes again
But the seas within were calm
And held me up
And carried me gently back to shore
Cement boots and all.
I was so ready to drown again.

(n.t., n.d.)

He didn't leave his apartment in time to see,
In the distance down Hollywood,
The sun set into re-runs
But he knows that it happened.
The boys fall across the street, his face a
Self-portrait by Picasso on a
Very self-loathing day—
Blue Period indeed.
He is ignoring all the warnings
And is operating heavy machinery—his psyche.
No one would call him beautiful,
This boy waiting for a bus,
But tonight the fates have done a line
And tonight the planets have aligned
And tonight he's feeling sexy
Poured straight up into Levis
Sweaty jockstrap holding everything in place
Just right.
He promises himself that he will enjoy the ride.
The iron horse gallops past neon tumbleweeds
Past men in thrift-store tweeds.

BIMBO

I just want to be pretty and inscrutable
And move around on airplanes
And drink coffee in someone else's town,
Then fly away like dust.
I like it when you tell me what to do
But don't really make me work
And give me lots of money
And tell me that you love me
But make me really feel it.
You can start on bended knee
And move on down from there.
I like cheap hotels and expensive strangers
And jacuzzi nights under desert stars
Naked with a cowboy
I found fixing his pick-up truck.
I can't remember what his name was
But I know that it was love
Or at least it was Palm Springs.
Today the mountains unrolled purple for me
But everything seemed easier in New York:
Elevators and fireworks and midnight cab rides,
"I've got the money" throbbing in my head.
So take the long way through the park.
I have seen the embers dying
In a Tijuana hooker hookah
And I was not particularly afraid.
I remember airports and confusion;
I was glamorous behind sun glasses
And in my mind a full-length fur
I want to wear my whole life
Slung low down on the shoulders.
Why have I wasted so much time
Trying to be a wife when those
Silly boys just want a mistress?
I know I am a nasty fuck
So I could have saved a lot of energy.
I have spent many nights alone.
I have an anthem in me,

Just like Helen Reddy.
I have a hairball of words
Hanging down in my throat
Where the tonsils used to be.
I'm just waiting for the gumption
To hack that bastard up.
Until then, I'll let someone else
Do the talking
And I'll just pose for pictures.

MY CATS IN AUGUST

My cats stretch out all of August
In the afternoon. In front of a dedicated
Fan, they are cat from nose to tail:
Bisecting the floor or table,
Sprawling beneath the bed,
Channeling brown queen River Nile,
Dreaming of Africa or perhaps of sunshine
Streaming through the windows in Chicago
Where the furniture was so much nicer.
And where we had air conditioning.
Kate knocks a box of envelopes to the floor,
Is startled, but goes quickly back to sleep.
My cats pull August like it was taffy
And want to donate their coats to PETA.

DAWN TELLS IT LIKE IT IS

It dawned on me
While I was waiting
For the bus
That I am twenty nine.
This was not a tender, gentle, rosy dawn;
It was a nuclear dawn,
A get your lazy ass out of bed
Motherfucker dawn.
It was a too many Jagermeisters,
The night before and you don't

Know the name of the guy
In bed next to you dawn.

I actually knew a girl
Named Dawn. She was a
Bitch, which I've never held
Against a person, but she
Was mean on top of it.
Anyway—this dawn—this
Dawn of realization—29,29,
29—and your mother still buys your underwear
And you work in a sex club:
This dawn was not a dawn
That softly focused on the
Chirping, waking birds and
Let you luxuriate in the
Smell of eggs and bacon and
Freshly squeezed orange juice—This was
A be grateful for your
Diet Coke and Pop Tarts dawn—
A fry those obnoxious fucking
Birds dawn—A dawn that was
Angry and had things to do and
Had no time for slow pokes—
A bitter and resentful dawn—
Bitter and resentful for
Being dragged into some piece
Of poem shit that was being
Written at 10:15 at night.
"Use the moon, motherfucker," this
Dawn seethed. "Haven't you heard of
dusk, poetry boy," this dawn raved.
I tried to tell her that
"It dusked on me" made
No sense, but she spat at
Me and continued with her
tirade. "I am the queen
Of dawns. I am the never ending
Dawn. I am the dawn you
Don't want to run across in

An unlit alley. I ride
The chariot of the Gods across
The Heavens, and your lazy, 29-year-old
Faggot ass is sitting in front
Of Le Bar at Sunset and
Thirtieth waiting for the
Bus. The goddamn Hollywood bus at that.
You're 29 and you ride the
Bus, so don't go dragging me
Into your lame-ass, weepy, horseshit
Poem about what a shock
It is to turn 29. Guess
What, genius, do the math; 30 is just around
The corner, and unless you
Have a better address and
A car, don't even think
Of alluding to me when
You write the inevitable
Poem about the horror
Of reaching that milestone."
And with that she hurled
Her Thierry Mugler orange-dyed
Mink stole around her neck.
"Fashion has nothing to do
With thermometers," she hissed
As she caught my sweaty stare, turned—
Scarlet petticoats flashing beneath
Her pink satin skirt—and moved quickly
And violently down the street
In a manner quite fitting
A malevolent, short-tempered force
Of nature.

THE IT'S ALRIGHT MAN BLUES

It's another week of Sloppy Joes, kids.
Yeah, it's another week of Sloppy Joes.
Daddy's trying to do his best,
But it's another week of Sloppy Joes.

It's another night on the floor, dear.
Oh, it's another night on the floor.
Your sugar's arms are still right here,

But it's another night sleeping on the floor.

It's another day off from my dreams, man,
Another fucking day off from my dreams.
Believe it or not, the rent's been paid,
But it's another day sleep walking from my dreams.

Yeah, it's the same shit on the table
And the same shit on the floor,
But I got two packs of smokes
And five cans of Diet Coke.
And it's alright, man.
And I've got a CD player
And I just took a hit of killer weed.
And it's alright, man.
And I'm crying in my Sloppy Joes
Cuz Marianne Faithfull is singing 'bout a woman
Who has lost all of her blessings.
And I thank every God I have ever done a shot with.
And I know my future's in the meat cooking
And the answers are all lying on that floor.
And it's alright, man.

OUR FRIENDLY ANIMAL KINGDOM—
A DOKUMENTARY

L.A. is not maternal;
She has her litter every year
Merely through force of habitat.
She leaves the crying cubs
In a den cleaved from barren rock—
The TV blaring for their company—
And attacks the city quietly.
She knows her children have to eat.

Her victims are old or sick or wounded
And never hear her coming.
Witnesses report silence and then a flash,
A terror and a slash of flesh.
The prey—dead—is dragged so quickly
Through the underbrush from which the demon came
That no one, not even the prey himself
Can remember that he even lived.
When mother returns, the crying cubs stop in mid-howl,
Mouths frozen open, once needing, now knowing
Dinner is served. Mama L.A. licks the blood
From her paws and the blood from her chops.
Smiling, eyes closed, she reclines and remembers,
Tasting this blood, when the victim was first born.

(n.t., 8/15/97)

I'm not pretty anymore.
Don't know what you call me for.
You got my number, think you can score.
Gave you my number; must have been bored.
Did you know I was a whore?
Gonna let the phone keep ringing
And spin here on the floor.

(n.t., 8/27/97)

I'm a queen who is King of Denial.
I'm a fag who can forget anything.
Unpleasant? Ignore it.
Distasteful? Just store it away.

(n.t., 8/27/97)

I'm a mess, but my dishes are clean.
Anger, seismic, makes the plates in my head shift:
Erupts mountains through the skin
On the back of my neck. Anger boils,
Angry boils—whatever. My kitchen
Has never looked so clean. Bitter tears,

Wrung out through the dish rag,
Hit the soapy water and cling to the soaking dishes.
Dawn gets out the grease,
But what about broken dreams?
I want to hurl the plates and glasses
At the thankless, unforgiving walls;
Want to hear the silverware
Do a desperate tap dance
On the floor that has grown jaded
To the doleful whimpering of tears,
And blood, and other human fluids.
Instead I punish them with cleanliness.
Oh, do not think you can just rest there
In the dishrack. Out, out damned waterspot.
Get thee to a cupboard.

(n.t., n.d) *

We arrived by U-Haul in a moment before
Night realized she was dying. My mother
Panicked when she saw the grey linoleum.
It was late; it was late August. They gave
Me the largest bedroom—to make me happy
About the move, I suppose, although
I don't recall being unhappy about the move.

* Revisiting the 1978 family move to Fayette.

I AM NOT THE BOY YOU THOUGHT I WAS

I scared a little old lady on the street tonight.
I didn't mean to, but I did.
She called me, "Son of a bitch,"
And it felt good.

(n.t., n.d.)

The litterbox is full of much too easy metaphor
And cleaning it is the apex of futility;

But I scoop away knowing the cat, like life,
Will have to shit again and prefers a clean receptacle.

(n.t., n.d.)

Humanity saunters 'round,
His pants unzipped,
And tries to look alluring.

Humanity plays with his cock,
Flopping from his grey shorts,
As I try hard not to giggle.

Humanity has not heard
That I am reclaiming my virginity.

Humanity plants himself next to me
Wearing nothing but a white oxford
And a cock ring.

He belches, does not say excuse me,
And has no idea that I'd like nothing more
Than to stub my dying cigarette out
On his ugly, flaccid prick.

I swear I did not look,
But how could it be otherwise?

Humanity is old and black and oriental,
And cracked and tired and white,
And young and boring, and sometimes beautiful;
But always very desperate.

SENSELESS

I finally figured out what it is I need.
I need a seeing-eye man—
Obedient, muscular, calm, cool and collected.
Oh Lord, send me a German shepherd.

Baaaaaa! Oh Lord, I can't see.
I won't put you in a harness—
Only hold my hand and help me cross the street.
Tell me when it is safe, guide me to the other side,
Show me my true reflection.
I need an ophthalmologist.
Make me wear coke bottle glasses.
I will abandon vanity if you will only make me see.

I am helpless in the world of vision.
I have been blinded by the glare of reality and taxes.
My sight has been clouded by airheads.
There was that nasty accident in the gym.
It is always fun until someone loses an eye.
Behind the glare there is darkness just as startling.
And I have to open my eyes as wide as they will go
To try to take it in—to try to comprehend the lights are on.
I know the lights are on.
I'm obsessive-compulsive; I checked.
The lights are on, but I'm sitting in this world of darkness.
I want infrared vision.
I want the words to describe the darkness.

Oh God, I am mute too.
I open the sphincter muscle of my mouth
As wide as it will go—the giant vortex of communication—,
And strain and force and pray.
I pray some word—any word—will fight its way up
From the prison of my inner being—
Up through the lungs and trachea—,
Claw through the dust and smoke and ashes—,
Attach itself to some motivated hunk of phlegm
And come spewing out into this waiting, wondering world,
And explain what it is I mean when I say that I am blind.
Can't you see I cannot see? I cannot function.
Where is my "Handicapped" hang-tag
So I can park in the spaces right in front of the library?
Oh yeah, that's right. I DO NOT HAVE A CAR.
I will lie down in the "Handicapped" parking space,
Wait to be run over, sue, win, buy a car or two.

And then you will give the hang-tags and the stickers,
And it will be recognized that I am senseless.

TALKING TO NIGHT ABOUT GOD AND MAN

Night knows that he will never love me,
Yet she is amused when she hears me saying
To myself—over dishes—I love him more now
Than when I thought I was in love with him.
Night listens, and smiles and drinks her coffee black.
I am doing dishes, talking to myself, gesturing
With dishpan hands, flinging bubbles of joy around the room

In my exuberance to make my point as Night,
Having let herself in—she never knocks, you know—
Is drinking her coffee and smoking. Night,
Fastidious by nature, never drops ashes on
Her long white gown; The possibility
Has never even crossed her mind
And she always finds an ashtray.
I keep on talking to myself, sequencing from
Love of a man to love of The Man.
"Oh, Night, I have found God," I yell
Over the roaring rush of water
Pouring from the violent faucet.
Night can only roll her eyes at this
Little bit of news. And to change the subject quickly
She exclaims quite brightly, "Dear,
Your incense is quite exotic!"
While thinking to herself how she has—
In her lifetime—seen quite a change
In the diet of poor poets:
> A meager roach
> Stolen from his boss's ashtray,
> Pop tarts, diet coke and cigarettes
> Are hardly astinthe* and opium
> But perhaps that is for the....
> Oh, no, no, no, I wouldn't go that far.

"Night, why are you shaking your head like that?"
I holler from the kitchen.
"Just fluffing out the curls, my dear."
Night is always on top of things.
"I'm really horny tonight, Night...."
    "Oh, my!"
"...And I thought I'd give him a call
And propose really nasty, pounding phone sex."
"Who, God?"
"No, the man I love more now than when
I moved across the country for him."
    "Not that he ever asked you to."
"Not that he ever asked me to."
"I'd stick to God right now if I were you,"
Was Night's succinct response.
    *unknown drug?

MICHAEL'S V.M.

It was a pop-song moment on my bed,
Phone to my ear, as you said,
"I wish you didn't live so far away
So I could crawl beside you
Hold you tight, just fall asleep."
The cool, crisp California night
Turned tricks outside the windows
As freight train whistles looked on in horror
From the distance.
"It's just Los Feliz*, dude.
Get your ass in your car, dude—
You got a car, dude—
And get on over here.
I'll give you all the holding you need."
But I didn't give you no sass.
I just purred, "Oh, baby."

* Los Feliz is an L.A. street.

INCLINED, RECLINED

Maybe it's slowly creeping over me,
This peacefulness,
Pouring over me like paint
In the hands of a slapstick comedian.
Turn the camera to slow-mo.
I need to feel peace creep among my capillaries,
And receptors need to feel pinpricks of calm
Dance up and down my spine.
I need to feel life tingle
In my thumbnails and my toes.

I have crawled cross beds of nails;
I have crawled across fields of glass.
I have seen blood flow
As I consciously dragged my knuckles,
I have seen blood cover calluses
Caused by hammering and smashing
Nails and glass....And now I'm
Sitting in a chair realizing that Peace
Could just walk—could just walk—through that door
At any moment, on its own accord.

Maybe Peace is key-hole tiny
And blew whispered in with wind and dust
And I never knew that it arrived
Until it decided that it was safe
To seep and creep and prick through skin
And cover my body from my toenails
To my thumbs.

(n.t., 12/22/97)

I am living my 8th or 7th life
In third-world Silver Lake,
The traffic and congestion—
Like movie reels from foreign countries.
Furniture and clothing for the war zone

Are sold on every corner
Hipsters walk around.

The woman waiting next to him
Asks if he could hear her screaming
Or if the screams are only in her head.
He said, "I only heard you laughing to yourself,
But should I be prepared?"
She didn't find it funny, told him he's a freak,
And moved over to the next bench.

He is early and he panics,
So he buys a beer and waits
In a bar with antique fixtures,
And men who are just as old,
And men who are just as fixed.
He drinks that cold beer quickly;
He is afraid he will be late.

(n.t., n.d.)

The steps to my apartment
Know that I'm a slut.
Thousands of bricks have just seen me
Stumble-float from the back of a cab,
Rock-'N-Roll courtesan, kissing
Another year good-bye.
Keys snicker in my trembling hand
As I try to find the right one.
"An appropriate metaphor, baby,"
They sneer, jagged, gleaming hallway hallogen.
I remember a tunnel of lights from the cab.
Traffic lights tumble to the ground.
Trucks remind us how large they are.
You said a sunset made you cry today.
On Santa Monica, everyone stopped
And breathed blue and oxygen,
Exhaled the year with hope for
Golden clouds and warmth
Falling into purple and magenta.

Your sheets, patterned Inca warrior,
Light like summer in your room.
Even the air wanted to stay and cuddle
In lingered blue and grey and hazy gold.
On the edges—a filter—a reminder of
Captivity somehow—but oh so happy in the cage.
A tyranny of horny summer puddles on
Your stomach.
Your skin is cool.
My mouth is dry.
You make me want to do things I have never done.
You are going to Australia.
My mouth is dry.

I smoke in the back of the cab,
Torpedo up the river of kind night,
Take off my wet suit, glow and reflect,
Genuflect in peace, hold my babies
And flake you off my skin,
Pick you out from underneath my fingernails
As Summer teases me and twists
My nipples just like you did.

THURSDAY'S CHILD ON A SATURDAY NIGHT

I don't know why I don't listen when I say it's time to go to bed.
I don't know why I don't listen
When I say it's time to stay at home.
It's time to lie down, stay inside,
Save what's left of my money,
Save what's right for my pride.
Ain't no beer at 2:00 a.m. in this thirsty town.
Ain't no booze when you need it most.
Can't smoke in bars no more.
If that's a joke, I'd rather hack black lungs.
Ain't no man at 2:00 a.m. wants to hear me talk.
By 3:00 a.m., they don't even want to know my name.

By 3:00 a.m., they're all the same.
They're all the same—looking for a darker corner.
They're all looking for the freeway home.
My money says it's time to leave.
My patience is going too.
I flag a cab at the bus stop
And try to hear the lullabies
That linger between stoplights.

(n.t., n.d.)

Ran into this boy I used to want to know.
He said, "You're so formal,"
And touched me in the dark.
(Oh, don't make me kill you, whore.)
He asked, "Is it alright?"
I thought "Whatever"; but said "OK."
He asked, "Do you want to touch me too?"
I said, "Frankly, no." And he walked away
And wondered if it's appropriate
To praise the Lord in cuffs.

(n.t., n.d.)

Was I not listening?
Did you say you loved me?
My attention was elsewhere.
I was polishing my misery.

(n.t., n.d.)

Waiting for morning
In rooms tattooed with mirrored light,
Married men circle me like horny doves
And tell me I would be the one
If it were not for the rings hidden
In their trouser pockets—rings rolling
Back and forth with breath mints and with lint
Making contact from time to time
Through trouser pockets and underwear

Laundered by the little woman—with flopping,
Straining, married cocks searching for crumbs,
They coo, "I think about you all the time."
"That's so sweet." I smile.
"You wanna buy me a car?"

(n.t., n.d.)

Someday I want to be a man like you,
A one-night stand like you.
Someday I want to sit in cuffs,
All muscle with my shirt off,
And let the young man light my smokes.
Someday I want to cut the bullshit
And ask the young man home,
And act surprised and touched
When he says yes with no hesitation.
I want to watch the young man's denim ass
Glide down, slide down into the
Leather seat of my Mercedes,
And speed off into the hills,
Grinning broadly into the night,
Stroking eager, inner thighs.
I want to light the candles,
And fluff the pillows and the egos,
And offer beer or pot or coke
Before I fuck the present ass.
Someday I want to be like you.
Someday I want to let them taste the view—
Loosen them up with the sight
Of the dancing lights laughing
Down the hill, laughing out to sea.
Someday I want to let strangers spend the night
And move us down into the guestroom
Because I know the workmen
Are coming early in the morning.
I want to have more sex in the morning
And tell him how wonderful it was
To wake up in his arms, and buy him lunch,
And exchange phone numbers, and kiss

In front of his rundown apartment,
And wave as they unlock their front doors,
And accelerate into Saturday.

(n.t., n.d.)

I want to call you up
And invite you over
To listen to the storm hit.
I want to hold you under sheets
And wait for God's concerto
And listen to Bob Dylan
Before the real rains really come.
I can hear the wind rustle
Mini blinds in open windows.
Glass breaks somewhere;
One could not ask
For a better poetic metaphor.
Palm trees are whipping
The sky into a frenzy of submission.
The rain is going to pour and come.
The building throbs with night and anticipation.
I want to call you up and invite you over
To listen to the world end.
There is a silence building, growing,
Building futures, stock-piling grain.
I don't know if you can hear it
With me entwined around your body,
Covering your ears as I smother you with kisses.
There is a stillness in my heart.
I'm standing beneath a boiling, angry sky
Waiting for the rains to come.
Need some water for my crops.

(n.t., n.d.)

See your pictures in the 'zine
And you look real good:
Pale, blank faces

Black and white keen—
London boys cigarette lean.

London boys, wish you were here
Or we were there.
London boys seem real cool

If we had the dollars,
If we were only rich,
We'd take it to the plane,
Get out of our scene,
And make the switch.

(n.t. n.d.)

He spent everything he had in his pocket
And told the world to keep the change.
No one would ever call him beautiful—
This boy waiting for a bus.
But tonight the fates have done a line,
And the planets have aligned,
And tonight he's feeling sexy
Poured straight-up into Levis:
Sweaty jock holding everything in place
Just right;
Fourth-of-July fireworks in miniature
At the end of his cigarette.
A woman joins him on the bus-stop bench
And asks how long he has been waiting.
He says, "Years."
She nods and knows he is not kidding.

How does he get on the bus?
Where is he going?
Why?
What does he want?

He understands the lure of neon
And the power of cement-entrapped stars.*
And the tourists seem to have all the answers

Or at least the proper equipment
To record all the questions.
On the top of a building at the top of a hill,
A sign flashes; light bulbs twinkle,
Blink on-off and tease,
"Free Parking in Rear."
That sums up this city he thinks
When he heads for the bus stop
And the long journey home.

* Neon refers to theatre advertising and "entrapped stars" are found in the Hollywood "Walk of Fame."

(n.t. 4/14/98)

Is it too much to ask for new problems?
I'm tired of the ones that I've got.
I know that life will never be easy.
I just want a fresh way to rot.
Is it demanding to want a new Hell?
The one I am living is leaving me cold.
Is it presumptious to want different demons?
I want some new angst before I'm too old.

(n.t., 4/23/98)

I should learn some patience;
I should show some pity.
Who knows when it will be me
Stumbling through this city
Looking for a light;
Begging for a smoke;
Desperate for a human touch,
Nicotine, or conversation—
Anything to ease the pain?

(n.t., 4/30/98)

This is the town
Where no one looks at you.

And on the rare occasion
That someone does look at you,
I guarantee he will not
Or she will not
Like what she sees.

           (n.t., 5/3/98)

I used to be a drunk;
Now I'm just nuts in a bowl—
Crackers in a basket
At the end of the bar.
I used to be a lush;
Now I'm just a cherry
Waiting to be dropped
Into some impatient Manhattan
Or Cosmopolitan by some Betty
Whose tongue has devious plans
For my stem.

DIZZY ON THE DOG

I hear someone behind me talking.
Or is it the voices in my head?
Whichever—no one is answering.
Bus driver calls out street names.
The shaking black chick
Doesn't have the last quarter.
She's just going to the next corner.
Just take her to the next corner, man.
I can't watch her twitch.
Tonight is the night
I learned to doubt everything,
And then learned to doubt it again.
I laid with a man
Who ought to be a preacher.
He told me to move.
I said, "Get your knee off my hair, Havvard."
One stop, man, I just wanted one stop, man.

She shakes into the darkness
And the bus lurches on.
Maybe the preacher man
Can only love me when I'm leaving.
He can only breathe
When he sees the door knob in my hand.
I was dressed for redemption;
Now I'm just sweaty
And wondering if I smell.
And the bus lurches on.
Maybe I can only breathe when I'm leaving.
Maybe I love the feel
Of the door knob in my hand.
I should have given her that last quarter.
I should have slapped those crack shakes out.
I should have testified:
"Sister, I know exactly where you've been."
But she's already been swallowed
By some night, freebasing sidewalk.
We are each and everyone someone's addiction.
We are each and everyone
Someone's long bus ride home.

VIII.

CRISIS, GRIEF, GUILT, & HEALING

Crisis

I was unusually vulnerable to bad decision-making in May, 1998. A pinched sciatic nerve forced me to sit down every five minutes. My wife, Carol, who had been born in England and had booked a walking tour there, was extra tense as her trip departure neared. (I was worn down by her increased insomnia, long-distance phone calls to England in the wee hours, and worrying about travel arrangements.)

She dreaded riding a shuttle van to the St. Louis airport—even with her trip companion. The last time she had taken a van to St. Louis by herself, she had a nervous collapse and was taken by ambulance for emergency testing. So I was to drive them both, then play in a bridge tournament in Illinois—followed by more vacationing.

Over decades, Carol's stress caused her to give up playing bridge and driving. She panicked during thunder storms, hated being alone, hyperventilated in traffic jams and when crossing bridges, plus making several hypochondriac phone calls a day. (Thirty-odd years ago she had stopped taking tranquilizers, and had thereafter refused stress counseling.)

On a Friday, two days before we were leaving, I phoned Rob who sounded pleasant and normal. (I agreed to send him $400 for rent.) When I asked how his job search and auditioning were going, he said that he'd been ill for several days. Fearing AIDS or TB, I was aghast; but he told me not to worry since flu, consistent with his symptoms, was "going around."

I pleaded with Rob to seek immediate medical care. In the sternest warning I ever gave him, I stressed the need for prompt treatment of certain diseases. Thinking he would have easy access to a free clinic, I urged him to go at once. I also suggested a call to a social worker he knew and/or the AIDS hotline.

Calling back Saturday morning, I was horrified that Rob had not gotten medical care. He sounded upbeat, however, and I did not sense that he was severely depressed—unable to make responsible health decisions. Again, I implored him to get medical attention. Suspecting that he was seriously ill, I considered options.

(1.) If I flew to L.A. immediately, Carol would cancel her England trip and accompany me—upsetting her companion from Columbia and her sister who would join them in St. Louis. (There was no chance that Carol would proceed with her trip, and await developments.) If she learned of my trip to L.A. while she was in England, she might well break down flying to join me, as she had done at the St. Louis airport.

(2.) If I put her on the England flight, cancelled my motel reservations in Illinois and flew from St. Louis to L.A., she would become distraught if she couldn't phone me in Illinois. After a frantic call to our son Mike in Orlando, her trip would be ruined and she would probably fly back as soon as possible.

(3.) If I asked Rob's friends in L.A. to help get him to a physician, he would resent my interference and perhaps be less likely to seek care. (Rob had made clear that he didn't want my advice or interference in his life. I hadn't been able to persuade him to quit smoking, get a job skill or meal-ticket degree, seek counseling and HIV testing, secure employment that included fringe benefits, and pursue all options to win acting roles. He flatly refused to accept or consider my list of West Coast acquaintances who were actors, directors, and employers. An old, comic line was applicable: "Mother, please, I'd rather do it myself.")

I spent the worst night of my life mulling alternatives. Much as Carol wanted to take her trip, I decided that there should be no balancing of interests between parents and son if a human life was threatened. But I wasn't sure that was the case.

What if Rob only had the flu and was recovering? Should I wreck Carol's trip by doing what I wanted to do—fly immediately to L.A.? Rob talked to Carol before we left and assured her that he was fine. She believed him and didn't worry about his health while she was gone. He told me that he felt "much better." I had my doubts, but decided not to alarm Carol. So, I drove Carol and her companion to St. Louis, continued to Illinois, and monitored Rob's condition with daily phone calls.

Rob did go to a clinic soon after, was diagnosed with flu, and sent home. A second visit, however, led to his hospitalization on Thursday. (If I had flown to L.A. the preceding Saturday, he might have been hospitalized four or five days sooner—if Rob and the medics had cooperated.)

In Illinois, I got a phone call from Carol, who was so worried about her health that she spoke in whispers. Assuming that she wouldn't call again for a few days, I cancelled my plans to drive further east, and concocted a strategy to cover my tracks while I went to L.A.

When a social worker at L.A. County Hospital phoned that Rob had been admitted, I called Mike and asked him to tell Carol that I was touring the Ozarks with friends I chanced to meet, that we couldn't be reached by phone because we were camping out. When I explained the reasons for this deception, he agreed to play along. Carol eventually called him, believed my alibi, and thoroughly enjoyed her trip.

I then drove to St. Louis, and flew to L.A. the Sunday before Memorial Day. Walking the hospital's long halls with directional lines painted on the floor, I met one of Rob's college room mates. She told me that his cell count was way down—an AIDS symptom, although full test results wouldn't be available till Tuesday. After I donned protective gear, I followed her into an isolation room.

It was shocking to see Rob in bed sustained by IVs and an oxygen mask. His hair was very dirty, and he needed a shave. Rob's other college room mate—who'd let him stay in her apartment when he was touring in L.A.—sat beside him. There was a good spirit in the room. All three were pleased to see me, and tacitly invited me to take charge.

I grabbed Rob's arm, shaking and patting it. (Whatever happened, I would never reproach him for his self-destructive lifestyle—fully revealed in his journals—and not contacting me when he first became ill. Nor would I tell his friends that they should have kept me informed.) Although he feared I would not like living with his cats, Rob offered to let me stay in his apartment, and politely asked whether I had mailed the check for his rent. (I had, and it later turned up in his mailbox.) He was serene and positive.

I promised to speak to the nurses about getting his hair washed. When I said I would get him an electric razor, one of the women offered to buy one on that day's shopping trip. I gratefully gave her enough money.

After explaining how matters stood with his mother, I asked whether he wanted me to phone her and invite her to come to L.A. He thanked me for the offer with a gentle smile and said, "No." But he winced when I said I'd have to meet her plane in St. Louis in two weeks. His benefactress touched his arm and he seemed to realize that my errand in Missouri wouldn't preclude returning to L.A.

To my surprise, everyone joined in when I launched a jocular conversation. Rob played along by asking about my news articles for the Columbia Tribune. He smiled when one of the women described her successes as a school teacher. (It was the smile of a mother holding her new-born child, an open window into a soul suffused with love for another human being, as simple and pure as the soul revealed in a shy school girl's smile when fondling her pet rabbit.)

When the benefactress prepared to leave, I induced her to drive me to a grocery and then to Rob's apartment. I told Rob that I would be back early the next morning to read poetry to him. He needed the oxygen to breathe, so I suggested he save strength by not talking very much. As I left, he called "I love you." I responded with a choked "Mutual."

I have wondered how I might have bettered this sad reunion. I already knew that Rob was hypersensitive. I became more aware of how deeply small slights wounded him by reading his journals. One night when Rob and a male lover were utterly drunk in a bar, the lover left the table without explanation. Given the circumstances, there could have been many explanations for the lover subsequently leaving the premises. But Rob was humiliated and bitterly hurt because the lover did not rejoin him.

The 3:00 a.m. phone call to Rob's apartment was terse. "He's going to intensive care. Please pick up his possessions." Before my cab arrived, I sank to my knees and pounded the bed with both hands, sobbing till my ribs ached. The crisis was not over, but the grieving had begun.

When I broke down again after they wheeled him away to I.C., a woman doctor asked if I wanted to hear her prognosis. I told her I thought Rob had AIDS and was terminal; she said they could treat him. She meant to be kind, but I thought she was peddling false hopes. I dubbed her the "sunshine doctor."

Visitors didn't have to wear protective gear to visit Rob in I.C. His hair was clean and trimmed, and he was shaved every day. Kept alive by intubation, he wrote responses or nodded his head when he was conscious. The worst moment was his lung collapse. (His nurse warned me that they would have to cure the AIDS, cure the double pneumonia, and then grow new lung tissue.)

There were happy-sad moments. When the "sunshine doctor" asked Rob whether he wanted to get out of I.C., he responded with a joyous, hopeful smile, revealing a beautiful, gentle spirit. When I reviewed all the people who loved him and were pulling for him, he wrote, "I am very blessed."

The best moments were poetry readings. Because it was so difficult to read aloud, I practiced "Isle of Innisfree," by William Butler Yeats. After reading Rob that poem, which contains a striking line about finding peace, he sighed contentedly and lapsed back into his coma. Hopefully, he had found peace.

The potentially most melodramatic moment of my I.C. interlude never occurred. Rob wrote that he wanted to hear Stevie Smith's "Not Waving but Drowning"—the poem that he said would explain so much about his life (See "Saugatuck"). When I found it, he was sedated into a continuous coma. It was so apropos, and piercingly sad, that I could not have read it to him without breaking down.

The I.C. days were much the same once Rob's coma was continuous, but there were some tough chores before I left to meet Carol's plane. I took his incontinent cat to be euthanized, crammed his writings into my suit case, and contacted a cremation association. On a fool's errand, I took the pennies he had hoarded to exchange for bills. Limping along, I looked over the rooftops and saw the HOLLYWOOD sign, that had enticed him since childhood and figures in his poems. As I left his bedside for the last time, I kissed him goodbye.

Carol and her companion were tired but happy when they got off their plane in St. Louis; back in Columbia, they embraced at parting. When Carol and I got home, I told her about Rob. She was crushed and asked what we would do. "Wait here," I said. So she resumed her duties directing the Columbia College library till Rob died in mid-June. We took time off to walk together through some parks and public gardens, and tried to plan for the future rather than living in the past. Her closure was to read the loving greeting cards from Rob; mine was to produce this book. Later that summer we attended a memorial service that Mike arranged in Orlando.

I had told one of Rob's friends that I would return to L.A., and several relatives said that I should go back and stay with him while he clung to life. Carol would have insisted on going too; but she was absorbed in her work, and I decided we should stay put. Travel and finding accommodations in L.A. would be highly stressful. Frankly, it was heartbreaking to see how handsome and dignified Rob looked in his terminal coma. It would have been torture for me to spend helpless hours by his side, and probably worse for Carol. Under the whips of misery, I feared that I would do or say things I would keenly regret. Carol too would need to have some release for her emotions. Since we couldn't contact Rob in his merciful sleep, I didn't want to aggravate our suffering by making the trip.

Occasionally I think of one of Rob's college chums, an artist, who had done two portraits of him—one with a note on the back saying, "I love you." A nurse said that she had visited during his continuous coma and gazed sadly at him for a long time. To do that willingly shows that people are very different.

I had arranged for cremation before I left, with scattering of ashes in the Pacific Ocean. For her "closure," Rob's closest friend asked to dispose of his ashes; but I refused her. Although I gave her authority to dispose of Rob's effects and money to sustain his surviving cat, she never forgave me. We were not invited to the commemorative gathering his friends staged in mid-Missouri, and I received a scathing letter condemning my decisions and severing future contact. But the crisis was over.

Grief & Guilt

I started grieving when Rob went to I.C. Back home, I painted the exterior of our home and did yard work after taking Carol to work—taking breaks to walk around the block with tears dripping down my face. Soon guilt kicked in.

Why hadn't I left immediately for L.A. when I learned that he was sick? Should I have taken Carol to L.A. to await the end? During many replays of Rob's early phone calls about his illness, I recalled that he had said that he was having trouble breathing. Shouldn't that have been enough to jump start me to L.A.? Father's Day had been horrible because I kept reminding myself that I wasn't in L.A. for him. I reviewed his entire life trying to pinpoint where I had gone wrong.

I focused on the things we did that seemed to be in his best interest, particularly those related to health and emotional balance. The alternatives to our choices were not guaranteed to succeed. What, for example, would have resulted from the counseling his school recommended for his "feminine behavior"?

When I couldn't identify a major, wrong decision, I turned to general issues of upbringing and support. Judging from his last nine years, I hadn't developed a strong moral character in him, nor taught him sound work habits. (But for 20 years, he was a good citizen, and strongly self-motivated in his schoolwork and theatre activities.) Clearly I hadn't achieved good father-son communications, nor done enough to get him established in Chicago and L.A.

Every time I concluded that I had acted well, I recalled the auto-safety expression, "You can be dead right, but you're still dead." Believing that my decisions were right couldn't change the fact that Rob was dead. (I often told myself, "Your son is dead." And I repeated this to my mirror.) I must be guilty because I had had control of a loving, sensitive, talented son in superb health. I must have failed to exhaust the possibilities for preventing his self-destructive conduct and early death from a preventable disease.

I recalled holding young Rob's wrist between my two front fingers with my thumb superimposed when we walked along busy streets.(My arm would be torn from its socket before my grasp was broken.) My swimming pool had a high fence around it, plus a lock no child could open. When we went to the Florida beaches, I made sure that he was safe. After age 20, however, I had neither control nor influence respecting his lifestyle. Although a parent should never give up, early training is obviously crucial. Why hadn't I anticipated Rob's problems that surfaced after age 20?

Healing

Healing doesn't mean that you don't have scars, or recurring aches. It means that you try to meet the legitimate needs of your deceased son's relatives, friends and acquaintances, and promote causes and values that seem worthwhile. To do this effectively, you must have the will to live a joyful life and a mind-set that sustains positive activity free of resentment, negativity, and depression. Here's how I got there.

I've pondered the sardonic adage, "Half your life is ruined by your parents; the other half is ruined by your children." It follows that persons desiring a happy life shouldn't have children, and I have great respect for those who believe that and act accordingly. This principle is more compelling if we acknowledge that the best of lives beyond infancy include: physical pain, illness, loneliness, rejection, frustration, grief, bereavement, acceptance of your eventual death, and death itself. How can one justify purposely creating another human being, who never asked to be born, yet will suffer dreadfully?

Consider an analogy. Suppose you saw a TV ad from an animal shelter showing a newborn puppy whose eyes were not yet open. It will be put to sleep that night unless someone assumes ownership within six hours. If you claim the puppy, you anticipate more personal pleasure than pain in raising it. But you aren't doing the puppy, who would suffer little if any by not waking up the next morning, any favor. He owes you nothing for giving him a chance for stomach cancer and/or getting hit by a car. He has the moral right to make his life choices, and disappoint you by running away, fighting, chasing cars, and biting strangers. It's your responsibility to preserve his life and good health; but if he's lost, you should focus on shared good times. (That's why you took him in and nurtured him.) Then use your experience positively.

Although most human births are probably unplanned, having Rob was a conscious decision. We wanted another child and took our chances. (He could have had serious birth defects, and no chance for a happy life.) He had no say about being born or how he was treated in infancy. Yet our culture has illogically made long-term gratitude and obedience to parents into duties, and considers suicide a sin. At majority, however, a competent human being has the moral right to control his own life or death so long as he doesn't physically injure the lives, liberties and property of others. Parents accordingly have no moral justification for pressuring their children's choices regarding careers, sexual preference, or place of residence. If a son flouts his prior parental training and squanders his talents, ruins his health, or terminates his life, his parents should numb themselves to those unpalatable realities and seek comfort in whatever joys he brought them. Otherwise parents may ruin at least half of their children's lives and the children can reciprocate. (At a child's majority, both generations should become autonomous.)

We supported his "marriage" and never reproached him for the nine bad years that anguished us. So we won't let Rob ruin the rest of our lives. He wouldn't want to cripple us. (He was afraid that we would be hurt by his homosexuality, and so relieved when we were not. In his final illness, he hoped that he would not spoil our vacations and that I would not be afraid when I came to visit him.) I am grateful to him for 20 great years together and for many insights into living my life to better advantage.

Just enjoying Rob as he grew up didn't change me much for the better. In fact I grew smug over his academic and acting successes, plus the recognition he received for citizenship and leadership. It was fun to read to him, open up the backyard pool for him and his friends, go to parks and the beach, attend plays and pop music performances, play board games or travel, and see him develop a wide circle of friends. I thought I had spent a lot of time with my son to good effect.

Rob taught me that it was O.K. for father and son to hug and say, "I love you." I'm glad that I did both and told him that I was proud to have him as my son. Through him I found how incredibly sensitive certain people are. Now I take exceptional pains to show respect and appreciation for others; I've even quit criticizing my bridge partners at the table. His poems and journals showed me how complex people are, that people who do vile things may have altruistic aspirations and a strong sense of right and wrong. (I had scoffed at a priest who told students at the University of Florida during the decadent 70s that they could retain "spiritual virginity" or "spiritual purity" despite their sins. This assertion had seemed to subvert morality just as the shameless grade inflation eroded academic integrity. Now I accept the concept of "spiritual purity.")

Most importantly, Rob's journals and poems showed me how much he loved and needed love—even from his pet cats—and how deeply he felt his triumphs and rejections. The journals showed that he had far more joy in his life that his poems alone would suggest. I think these materials are a solid contribution to the humanities, and I want to share them. They helped me see literature and biography in a fresh light: as sources for my ongoing healing and inspiration for my own creativity.

Rob's high-school journals showed that he didn't truly fit the Stevie Smith situation of finding life "too cold always." Helping direct the junior high play elated him. Rob was so grateful to his English teacher, who wrote so many supportive and witty comments into the journals, that he gauchely offered to counsel his mentor if need be. He was ecstatic to find that he was attractive to the other sex. (Girls from three neighboring towns—acquaintances from speech contests—invited him to their school plays.) It's comforting to find that he wasn't simply a wretched acne-case enduring a joyless existence.

He didn't grow up believing that acting was an easy way to make a living, or that it was the only thing he could enjoy doing. It's undeniably true that he later hated ordinary work; but he had exemplary study habits, committed himself to acting and speaking well, and did household chores with a right good will. Since he was preparing for defined goals, I saw no need for him to have part-time jobs. Because of the danger involved, I never asked him to run the power mower. When he recorded this fact in his journal, the English teacher commented, "You haven't missed a thing." Right on! I can't see that Rob would have been better off doing odd jobs than reading.

Although Rob lied to us many times (from denying that he had bleached his hair as a child to saying that he was working in a L.A. bar toward the end of his life), and his poetry was frequently surreal, he told the truth in his journals—truths that hastened my healing. When he sadly left New York without much money after being dropped from the cast, he first wished that he had started hooking sooner—then corrected to a wish that he had gotten a supplementary "real job." In his final journal entry, he stated clearly who had ruined his life. He had!

Reading biographies furthered my healing by showing that self-destructive conduct happens in the best of families. John Adams grieved over the alcoholism and early death of his sweet-natured son, Charles. The list is so long that simplistic explanations based on heredity and cultural environment are vapid. Countless distinguished parents have asked themselves, "Where did I go wrong?" I may have failed the test of parenthood, but some of the greatest spirits in history have too. Perhaps parents should be judged by the quality of their efforts to give a child a chance for a happy life rather than by the child's career alone. As he matures, a child and the society he lives in should assume an increasing share of the responsibility for his choices and actions. Even so, parenting is excruciatingly difficult.

Rick Bragg, who doesn't want children of his own as a matter of principle, gave me some reinforcement in When the Shoutin' Stopped. His mother loved her mother deeply, but she did not attend her mother's funeral. Despite our culture's adherence to traditional funerals, I think Mrs. Bragg's decision should be respected. Anthony Quinn, for instance, did not attend the funeral of his daughter who drowned in his back-yard swimming pool. I feel justified in claiming the same latitude for deciding not to return to my comatose son's bedside in L.A., and denying his friend's request to dispose of his ashes. Finding out about other people's choices helped me understand my relationship with Rob, and dispelled some of my guilt.

Thanks to this enhanced experience of Rob, I have become a better family member. I have pitched a lot of tennis balls for my grandson to bat, took him to catch his first fish and score his first par on a golf course. Primarily for safety reasons, I bought Mike a new Chevrolet Lumina to replace the old, small car he was driving. After hosting a family reunion in Columbia, I was on the best terms ever with my brother and sister.

For Christmas, 2001, I sent a portrait of Rob and his L.A. benefactress to his beloved cousin in Texas. This reminded me of the best time we ever had together—driving from Texas to Missouri through the Ozarks. Both boys caught several large trout at a fish farm. We then took a guided horseback ride, enjoyed a cookout, and rode back through the twilight.

We still have a portrait of Rob, also by his college chum, in our living room. I wear his belt every day and still use the electric razor he never saw in L.A.

I deplore much of his lifestyle after age 20, but those choices were his to make. Since he didn't want to hurt us and I refuse to let him ruin my later life, I can't resent how much he hurt us. Nor do I bear grudges against his "friends," who did drugs and partied with him, and never warned us how desperate he became. They were adults and will suffer enough without my malice. Besides, the "friends" are irrelevant. Rob chose self-destruction. He, not they, plunged me into grief and guilt.

I can't be a better person if I am crippled with guilt, so I will keep fighting it. Doubtless my parenting could have been better, but he did achieve his dreams of excelling in college theatricals and touring the nation as a professional actor. He saw clearly what he needed to do to get a grip on life, and sometimes sought to achieve it.

Having said that Rob's final weeks in New York City were a melodrama with numerous subplots, his life was a romance—a quest for love and self-respect with many chances to follow his resolutions and take the path to stability. His passage from personal triumphs to total ruin demonstrates the complexities of human frailty.

I won't say that I'll take Rob "As Is." We went separate ways when he reached adulthood, and I now dwell exclusively on his positives. He was incredibly sensitive, easily hurt by slights or rejection, and tortured by fears of failure. I find ultimate solace in murmuring, "Nothing can hurt him now."

0-595-32623-4

Printed in the United States
23570LVS00006B/1-24